RAPE: CONTROVERSIAL ISSUES

RAPE: CONTROVERSIAL ISSUES
Criminal Profiles, Date Rape,
False Reports and False Memories

By

JOHN M. MACDONALD, M.D.

Professor Emeritus
Department of Psychiatry
University of Colorado Health Sciences Center

And a Chapter With

DAVID L. MICHAUD
Chief of Police
Denver, Colorado

CHARLES C THOMAS • PUBLISHER
Springfield • Illinois • U.S.A.

Published and Distributed Throughout the World by
CHARLES C THOMAS • PUBLISHER
2600 South First Street
Springfield, Illinois 62794-9265

© *1995 by* CHARLES C THOMAS • PUBLISHER
ISBN 0-398-06545-4 (cloth)
ISBN 0-398-06546-2 (paper)
Library of Congress Catalog Card Number: 95-20430

With THOMAS BOOKS *careful attention is given to all details of manufacturing and design. It is the Publisher's desire to present books that are satisfactory as to their physical qualities and artistic possibilities and appropriate for their particular use.* THOMAS BOOKS *will be true to those laws of quality that assure a good name and good will.*

Printed in the United States of America
SC-R-3

Library of Congress Cataloging-in-Publication Data

Macdonald, John M. (John Marshall, 1920-
    Rape : controversial issues : criminal profiles, date rape, false
reports and false memories / by John M. Macdonald : with a chapter
by David L. Michaud.
        p.   cm.
    Includes bibliographical references and index.
    ISBN 0-398-06545-4 (cloth). — ISBN 0-398-06546-2 (paper)
    1. Rape.   I. Michaud, David L.   II. Title.
HV6558.M245   1995
364.1′532 — dc20   95-20430
                                                                          CIP

PREFACE

Rape is a terrible crime which arouses strong emotions. Opinions are sharply divided, especially on date rape, false memories of childhood sexual abuse, and false reports of rape. There seems to be no agreement on why men rape. The police have been criticized for insensitivity toward the victims, judges have been blamed for failure to send the offenders to prison, and the public has been requested to believe the children. Yet some children tell fanciful tales of Satanic rapes and murders. Does treatment work? These are some of the controversial issues on rape that will be reviewed in this book.

Interviews with over 200 rape offenders, including ten who killed their victims, and interviews with many victims have provided information not usually presented in research articles in professional journals. Both rapists and their victims help to convey some of the complexities of rape. In the first chapter a victim of rape and attempted murder describes her ordeal. Anyone who reads her account will never need to be reminded of the horrors of rape. In other chapters rape offenders describe their rapes and their backgrounds.

References additional to those articles or books quoted in the text are given in some chapters. These references have been selected because they contain original contributions or comprehensive reviews.

ACKNOWLEDGMENTS

I wish to thank the rape victims who talked to me at length about experiences they had no wish to recall. Psychiatrists, psychologists, lawyers, and detectives from many police departments have helped me. Attorney Craig Truman and psychiatrist Seymour Sundell reviewed selected chapters and I greatly appreciate their advice. Rape offenders have provided information about themselves that they would not readily reveal to others.

The Denver Police Department has long provided generous cooperation and assistance. Through permission to ride in police cars, I have gained useful information at crime scenes. Police Chief David L. Michaud has contributed to one of the chapters. Sex crime detectives who were most helpful include Lieutenant Curt Williams, Sergeants Dennis Cribari, B.J. Haze, and Tony Lombard, as well as Detectives Paige Lyda, Carrolyn Priest, Jim Burkhalter, Cleo Wilson, Bill Wickersham, Laura Tinnin, Chris Bridges, Frank Donlon, Avis Laurita, Jim Huff, Ervin Haynes, Darrold Hudley, Medardo Cisneros, Calvin Hemphill, Alex Wilson, and Amy Alonzo.

My thanks are due to many authors and publishers who have permitted reproduction of material. Permission to quote at length is greatly appreciated. For copyright purposes, the source of quotation has been listed, unless otherwise requested, under author, title, and publisher in the references at the end of each chapter.

CONTENTS

RAPE: CONTROVERSIAL ISSUES

Chapter 1

THE CRIME OF RAPE

For I must talk of murders, rapes and massacres
Acts of black night, abominable deeds.

Shakespeare, *Titus Andronicus*

WOMEN ARE NOT THE ONLY VICTIMS

Rape is one of the most despicable crimes. Abhorrence of rape is not confined to law-abiding citizens. Within penitentiary walls, inmates look down on the rapist and may assault or even kill him. It is a crime without honor. Armed robbers such as Robin Hood and Jesse James have become folk heroes. Thousands of mourners have attended the funerals of Mafia leaders. Many people express grudging admiration for colorful swindlers. But no one claims the rapist as a friend.

Yet there is disagreement on what constitutes rape. There are men who believe that when a girl, wearing a short dress, goes alone at night to their apartment, and drinks alcohol she is agreeing to sexual intercourse. There are men who think that when their date says "No," she really means "Yes." There are youths, fraternity students, and other macho males who think that when a girl at a party agrees to have sex with one of them, she agrees to sex with all of them.

There is sharp disagreement on the incidence of rape. Feminists are not alone in claiming that the motives for rape are not sexual but anger at women and expression of power over them. Controversial aspects of date rape, group rape, police response to rape, law enforcement profiles of serial rapists, resistance against rapists, and the role of the courts will be reviewed. The very sensitive issue of false reports of rape by women and children will be explored in depth. There is also a chapter on serial rape murderers.

The author of this book has interviewed over 200 rape offenders, including ten rapists who murdered their victims. He has also interviewed many rape victims and has been present when other victims were interviewed by detectives or by nurses from the Denver Visiting Nurse Service.

RAPE DEFINED

Rape is unlawful sexual intercourse with a female without her consent, or when consent is obtained by threats of violence; by deception, for example, by impersonating the woman's husband; or by the administration of any intoxicating substance. Women of unsound mind may be incapable of giving legal consent. Penetration of the vagina need not be complete, the slightest penetration is sufficient, and ejaculation need not occur.

Statutory rape is unlawful sexual intercourse with a willing female child under the age of consent. At present, the age of consent in American jurisdictions ranges from eleven to seventeen years. The age should not be so young that little protection is provided for a child, nor so late that a man can be held for statutory rape when the "victim" is fully capable of informed consent and readily acquiesced to a proposal or even invited a sexual relationship (Kourany et al.).

In the *Uniform Crime Reports* of the FBI, an important source of statistics, forcible rape is defined as the carnal knowledge of a female forcibly and against her will. Assaults or attempts to commit rape by force or threat of force are also included; however, statutory rape (without force) and other sex offenses are excluded.

THE INCIDENCE OF RAPE

Crime rates are usually based on the number of crimes per unit of population. By *Uniform Crime Reports*'s definition, the victims of forcible rape are always female. In 1993, an estimated 79 of every 100,000 females in the U.S. were rape victims. There were 84 victims per 100,000 females in metropolitan statistical areas, 76 per 100,000 in cities outside metropolitan areas, and 49 per 100,000 females in rural counties.

During 1993, there were an estimated 104,806 forcible rapes in the nation. Eighty-seven percent were rapes by force and the remainder were attempts or assaults to commit forcible rape. The actual number of rapes is much higher as many victims of rape never report the offense to the police.

The FBI has been issuing crime reports only since 1930. Ferdinand, in a study of the annual arrest reports of the Boston police from 1849 to 1951, found that murder, larceny, and assault had shown a clear decline; burglary and robbery had shown a downward tendency; and manslaughter had declined from initial high levels. Only forcible rape had shown a clear tendency to increase over that one-hundred-year period.

Forcible rape has continued to increase according to the *Uniform Crime Reports* of the FBI. In 1970, 36 out of every 100,000 females in this country were reported rape victims. In 1980 an estimated 71 of every 100,000 females, in 1990 an estimated 80 of every 100,000 females, and in 1993 79 of every 100,000 females were reported rape victims.

Some Other Statistics

In 1993, the greatest number of rapes were reported during the summer months. Thus July (9.7 percent) and August (9.3 percent) had the highest percentage of rapes. In contrast, November (7.5 percent) December (7.7 percent) January (7.7 percent) and February (6.9 percent) had the lowest percentage of rapes.

Nationwide in 1993, over half of the forcible rapes reported to law enforcement were cleared by arrest or exceptional means. About three of every ten arrested were in the 18 to 24 age group. Fourteen percent were under eighteen years of age.

THE TRUE INCIDENCE OF RAPE

The incidence of forcible rape is much higher than that recorded in official statistics. The *Uniform Crime Reports* note that rape is one of the most underreported of all Index crimes: murder, rape, robbery, aggravated assault, burglary, larceny-theft, motor vehicle theft, and arson.

FAILURE TO REPORT RAPE

Rape by a relative, friend, or date is less likely to be reported than rape by a stranger. The young girl who is assaulted by her mother's boyfriend may find that mother does not believe her or tells her not to notify the police. The mother would rather retain the affections of her lover than protect the welfare of her child. Stepfathers often escape prosecution in this manner.

As many rapists threaten to kill their victims, or the victims' children if they report the rape to the police, fear of retaliation is a factor. Arrest of the rapist does not preclude danger, as release on bond before trial commonly occurs. Furthermore, the offender may warn the woman that he has friends who will assault her if he is arrested.

The woman's shame may be so great that she does not mention the rape to anyone. The victim's wish to forget about the rape, to blot it from her mind and to get on with her life results in a decision not to notify the police.

On the other hand, ladies of easy virtue may not be greatly upset because some man takes her by force rather than by finesse. Some victims show such a casual attitude toward rape that they do not want to be bothered by the inconvenience of a complaint to the police. One woman came with her husband to a police station to report the theft of a record player. At this time the husband suggested that his wife should also report an attempted rape which had occurred one week earlier.

Fear of rejection by her husband or boyfriend may seal her lips. When the rape is the outcome of some activity forbidden by a parent or husband, the victim may not tell anyone; for example, the young girl who continues to associate with a boyfriend of doubtful reputation against the instructions of her parents, and the wife who goes to a drinking party while her husband is on service overseas with the Army may remain silent about the rape. Pregnancy leads to a belated report of rape to the police.

Fear of newspaper or television publicity may deter the victim from notifying the police. Editors sometimes show little sensitivity or discretion in their reports of the nature and circumstances of the sexual assault. A well-publicized sexual assault in which the victim's name was reported included reference to discovery of rocks in the vagina of the comatose victim.

Fear of embarrassment in the courtroom is another factor which may discourage victims from reporting the rape. Defense attorneys often attempt to save their clients from conviction and punishment by insinuating that the victim did not resist the assault or by attempting to discredit the moral character of the victim. Sometimes these insinuations lack any basis in fact. Many victims lack confidence in the criminal justice system.

Some parents of young victims fail to notify the police as the child's experience in the courtroom may be as traumatic as the rape, especially when the victim is unfairly attacked by the defense attorney.

FALSE REPORTS OF RAPE

False reports of rape which are not detected by the police may inflate rape statistics. The FBI *Uniform Crime Reports* list the number of unfounded reports of rape in the United States. Not all unfounded reports are false reports, but many are. A report may be unfounded by a police department because it occurred outside the city limits of that police department. In 1993, 8 percent of all rapes reported to the police were determined by police investigation to be unfounded.

A need for sympathy or attention, an attempt to maintain the affection of a boyfriend, an explanation for pregnancy while the husband is in jail or overseas, anger following rejection by a lover, and resentment by a prostitute over a client's use of force or failure to pay are among the reasons for false reports, which will be reviewed in Chapters 5 and 6.

A RAPE VICTIM DESCRIBES HER FATE

Legal definitions of rape do not convey the unbelievable horror and suffering that victims can experience. A young woman raped, stabbed, and left to die in a burning, smoke-filled, barricaded closet in her home told me about her fight for survival:

It was about 8:30 A.M.; I had just dropped my kids off at school. There was knock on the door. I looked out; it was Ronnie, the next door neighbor kid. I opened the door and he asked if he could use the phone. I told him "sure," and he headed upstairs toward the phone. He'd used it before and knew where it was. After three or four minutes he hung up the phone and headed for the door. He stood in front of it and asked what time my husband was going to be home. I told him around 7 o'clock that night.

He locked the front door and pulled a gun out of his pants. It was a small gun; I think it was an automatic and he pointed it at me. He said, "You have money, don't you?" I just said, "What" and he repeated the same thing, "You have money, don't you?" He pointed the gun at my face. I thought he was kidding so I just pushed the gun aside. I laughed and said, "No I don't have any money." He held the gun to the right side of my head and that's when I knew he was serious. He told me to go to my bedroom and sit on my bed.

He took some kind of cord and he tied my hands behind my back. Then he told me to stand up and he put a blindfold on my eyes and tied it in the back. Then he told me to open my mouth wide and I did. He took a sock and he ran it across my mouth, inside between my teeth, and he tied it in the back also. It was kind of hard to breathe because I was so scared. He told me to sit down on the bed and he said I was not to ask any questions; from then on he was going to ask me questions and I was just supposed to answer.

I could hear him rummaging through our dresser drawers and our jewelry box. He kept asking if this was it and I told him there was another jewelry box on the other dresser. Then he had me kneel against the bed and put my face on the bed and he stepped out of the room.

He got my purse from the living room and dumped it beside my head. He found my MasterCard and asked me what the code number was. I made up four numbers. He made me repeat them back to him and asked if they were correct. He said he would go to a Seven-Eleven store and if he found the numbers were wrong he would come back and kill me. Then he had me stand up and he said he couldn't believe this was all we had, and that I'd have to pay him some other way.

He pulled up my shirt and started grabbing at my breasts. I started yelling "No" at him and I jerked my body around and I went between the bed post and the mattress. Then he pushed me face down on the bed. He put the gun back to the left side of my head and told me to stand up. He undid my jeans and pulled my underwear and my jeans off at the same time. He had me step out of them and he asked me to get on the bed. I kind of kneeled on the floor and laid the upper part of my body on the bed. He couldn't get to me and he got mad. He told me he had better things planned and that we were going to go downstairs.

He had me stand up and led me to the front of the stairs. Then he nudged my shoulder and led me to step down on each step. In the den down stairs he had me lay down on the floor and he spread my legs apart. Then he inserted himself and asked me to fuck him. I told him I couldn't because my hands hurt me too bad, laying on my back with my hands tied behind me. When he finished he said, "It was good wasn't it?".

He told me to get up and to sit on the couch. I couldn't see it because I was blindfolded. He said I knew where it was and to find it. So I stepped till I felt my leg hit the couch and I sat on the couch. He started going up and down the stairs. He came back down and asked me to stand up again. He started putting duct tape around my face. He went round and round and all he left out was my nose. When he finished by wrapping it around my neck he started patting the tape down. Then he grabbed the side of my arm and pulled me to the crawl space, put me in and closed the door.

I kind of bumped around and tried to figure out where the door was by listening to him talk. So I faced where I thought the door was and started to undo my hands. I felt where one knot was and tugged at it, but it wouldn't come loose, so I felt for another knot. After I got the other knot loose I kept tugging and the rope came free. I held the rope behind my back. I figured if he came to the door I would try to choke him with it, but then I thought that being I can't see I'd probably miss and he'd kill me.

Then he opened the door and asked me where my hammer was. Then he came back and asked me where my suitcases were. I heard him going up and down stairs and it sounded like he opened the patio door. It sounded quiet for five to ten minutes so I thought he'd left. I opened the crawl space door and headed toward the steps. Before I even hit the steps I heard him run down the steps toward me. He hit me with a hammer on the right side of my head and I saw black real quick. Then I thought if I didn't act like he knocked me out he'd hit me some more, so I kind of fell to the floor.

He started asking me where did I think I was going. I just laid there and didn't answer him. He came behind me and started dragging me back in the crawl space. Then he opened the little crawl space door, took my legs and flipped me over a cement ledge back into the crawl space. He straightened my legs out then closed the door and the closet door in front of it. I heard him watching the TV and flushing the toilet. I tried to find the end of the duct tape on my face. I found the end on one side and got to go to the other side; then I couldn't move it anymore.

Then he came down and opened the doors again. He looked at me and I just laid there, but I think he could tell I was messing with the tape. He closed the door and went upstairs; then he came right down again and opened the doors.

He grabbed my right arm and cut it; I felt something sharp go across my wrist. He cut it about three times. I could feel his fingers touching me, so I thought it was a razor blade. He put my right arm down and grabbed my left arm. He did the same to my left wrist, cut it three of four times. Then he took my right leg and turned it to the side so my inner thigh faced him and he cut my thigh several times. I was acting like I was knocked out and I didn't scream or nothing.

Then he unplugged the light, closed both doors and went upstairs. I thought I have to get this tape off my face; I have to see how bad he cut me. I couldn't find the end of the tape. He came back down the stairs and opened up the doors. Then I felt something sharp on the left side of my chest. I thought, Oh my God, it's a knife, part of it went in me. I thought if I acted like I was still knocked out that he'd ram it through my chest and then I would be dead. So I reached up and grabbed for the knife and I got it the first time. I think I was able to do that because he thought I was still unconscious.

I started swinging the knife in the direction I thought he was at. I wanted to hit him with the knife. Somehow he got behind the crawl space door and he was leaning against it, because I was pushing and hitting the door and I could feel it move a little and it would close. I figured he'd head for the closet door so I waited a few minutes and I pushed on the crawl space door and it opened freely. Getting out of the crawl space I hurt my knee on the cement ledge and dropped the knife. I panicked and started feeling all around the floor for the knife. By the time I found it, I could hear him shutting the closet door.

He opened the door a little and asked for the knife back. I told him no, that he knew I had two kids and to take what he wanted and leave me alone. So I sat on the floor with the knife aimed at where I thought the closet door would be. Then I thought the best chance I had was to be able to see. So I took the knife and went under my neck and started sliding the knife under the duct tape, up and outward. I pulled the tape to the side of my face. The rest was all stuck in my hair.

Then he opened the door a little bit and asked me for the knife again. He said he wouldn't hurt me if I gave it back to him. I told him I wanted to kill him for what he did to me so he closed the door again. He said that was fine, he would just wait till I bled to death or passed out from losing too much blood because he was going to do what he was going to do. He knew that he had till 7 o'clock that night. I knew I needed to fix my wrists so I grabbed at the front of my shirt and cut two strips off to make tourniquets. I wrapped my wrists.

I heard him go upstairs and come back down; then I heard him hammering on the closet door. Then he pulled on it to see if it would come loose. He hammered on it some more; then he put a little wedge under the door, because I saw some of it come through. Then he moved something in front of the door (It was a large, heavy six drawer dresser). I heard him go into the bathroom, then into the linen closet. He was dropping things on the floor, so I figured he was grabbing the towels and bed sheets and putting them on the floor.

Then I heard some kind of spraying sound, like when you spray hair spray or something, you hear that psst, psst, psst. Then I heard a flicking sound like a lighter. He flicked it about four times. Then I saw a bright orange yellow glow and I thought he was trying to smoke me out or have me burn. The smoke was starting to come in. I knew most of the oxygen is near the floor, and I knew I had to start plugging up the door so the smoke wouldn't come in so bad.

I didn't want him to get away with it. So I started playing with the blood on my wrist and I wrote "Ronnie next door" on the side of the wall by the door. Then I thought if I don't get out because of this fire, it might burn up and nobody will know. So I went in the crawl space and found a little plug-in light. I plugged it in and turned it on. I wrote "Ronnie next door" on the cement ledge between the crawl space and the closet. I thought he'll see this also, so I wrote it on the side of a big box under the stairs, hoping he wouldn't see it.

The smoke alarms started beeping and I guess he turned them off. The smoke was coming in pretty good through the crack under the door. I found some old Halloween costumes and kids' toys in the boxes and I put them in front of the door where the crack was and I laid low to the ground. I heard a car engine in our driveway. I figured I needed to try to get out now. So I stood up to the door and rammed against it. It wouldn't budge. I took the knife and tried to bust open the water pipes, but all it did was scratch them.

I prayed to God and said I wasn't afraid to die, but I didn't want my kids and my husband to see me like that, and have that as their last memory of me. Something told me to get up and try the locked door again. I rammed at the door and it opened about six inches. The black smoke came in real good and started choking me. So I went to the ground and looked up right at the door knob. I saw something sticking out of the door frame. I touched it. It was real hot, so I knew I couldn't go over it. So I sat on the ground and pushed the door with my feet. The dresser went back and the door flew open. I headed toward the back of the house where my son's room was.

It was real black smoke, it was so black I couldn't really see and I was choking bad. I just knew where my kid's rooms were. When I got in my son's room I could see the outline of the window; the sun was probably shining through it. I stood up and hit the window with the handle of the knife, but it only made a hole the size of the handle and it cracked the window. I thought, Oh God, if he's still in there, he's going to hear this.

So I frantically started hitting the window as fast as I could till I knocked most of it out. I got on the window ledge and crawled out the window. That was right at ground level. When the air hit me it almost knocked me out.

I walked to the side of the house and peaked through the fence by Ronnie's house to see if I could see him. Then I felt I should go to the back fence. I got on the dog house and when I got on top of the fence I started yelling for help. I kept on yelling till I heard someone say they'd called for help. I jumped over the fence and stood on a little metal box and someone yelled at me to stay right there. I walked up to the back window of the house. They asked what happened to me. I told them my next door neighbor's son tried to kill me. Then I gave them my husband's name and work phone number and asked them to call him for me. They came back and said they did.

Nobody came out to help me. Nobody threw me anything. All I had on was the shirt that was torn. Later they told me I looked crazy, I was covered in blood and I had a knife in my hand. One guy testified in court later that he closed his windows so he couldn't hear me screaming. I just stayed on the side of the house till I heard the sirens get closer. I figured I needed to go to the front where they could find me. I was leaning forward trying to make my shirt cover my body. I went to the curb and I sat down. I set the knife on the right side of me so they wouldn't think I was going to attack them.

It was a fire truck and they asked me what happened. I showed them which house was mine. I told them it was on fire, that I had a dog in the garage, two hamsters and a rabbit upstairs and to please get them out. The firemen asked did he do that to your hand and knees?

That's when I found out I had cut my knees and toes on the window ledge and my hand when I banged against the window with the handle of the knife. I didn't remember feeling it. There were thorns and stickers from the yard in my feet and knees. My face and nose were black. I was in the fire so long it damaged my lungs, that's why I've got asthma.

Then the ambulance came. I asked the ambulance attendant what time it was and he said 10:20. I spent two days in the hospital. They had to repair the artery and two tendons that he had cut. I still have numbness on the side of my right hand.

Ronnie took all the jewelry, money, cameras, a video recorder, a stereo set, and suitcases from the home. He told the detective who arrested him in Oklahoma that he had been watching the victim for a long time and he had to have her. He left the stolen property in a dumpster and he asked a relative to recover it, dispose of it, and not to say anything to anyone.

[She had burn scars on her wrists and forearms as well as scars from the knife wounds on her wrists and right thigh. She also had scars from grabbing the blade of the knife. The fire melted the electrical wiring in her house and repairs took two months.]

EXPANDED DEFINITIONS OF RAPE

In some states, the definition of rape includes the rape of men by men. The *National Incident-Based Reporting System* (*NIBRS*) of the FBI, introduced in 1991, uses an expanded definition of rape. A preliminary report on rape in Alabama, South Carolina and North Dakota in 1991 listed 3,712 incidents for which the sex of both the offender and the victim was recorded. About 90 percent of these incidents involved a male offender attacking a female victim. About 9 per cent involved male offenders and male victims. Female offenders and female victims accounted for 0.8 percent and female offenders and male victims accounted for 0.2 percent of the incidents (Reaves).

WOMEN RAPING MEN

Malinowski in the *Sexual Life of Savages in North-Western Melanesia* describes violent sexual assaults on men by the women of Vakuta and some other southern villages. Women working together in the communal weeding of garden plots had the right to attack strangers from other villages passing within sight.

The man is the fair game of the women for all that sexual violence, obscene cruelty, filthy pollution and rough handling can do to him. Thus first they pull off and tear up his pubic leaf, the protection of his modesty and, to a native, the symbol of his manly dignity. Then by masturbatory practices and exhibitionism, they try to produce an erection in their victim and, when their maneuvers have brought about the desired result, one of them squats over him and inserts his penis into her vagina. After the first ejaculation he may be treated in the same manner by another woman.

Worse things are to follow. Some of the women will defecate and micturate over his body, paying special attention to his face, which they pollute as thoroughly as they can. "A man will vomit, and vomit, and vomit," said a sympathetic informant. Sometimes these furies rub their genitals against his nose and mouth, and use his fingers and toes, in fact, any projecting part of his body, for lascivious purposes.

Philip Sarrel, M.D. of Yale University and William Masters, M.D. of the Masters and Johnson Institute have reported three cases of sexual assault involving threats of physical violence by women on men who were forced to have sexual intercourse. Threats of castration and death were combined with penile stimulation so that the men were able to perform sexually despite their fear and humiliation. All three men subsequently became impotent.

A twenty-seven-year-old, 178 pound truck driver left a bar with a woman he had met for the first time that evening and went with her to a motel. After he was given a drink in the motel, he fell asleep. He woke up to find that all his clothes had been removed and he was tied hand and foot to the bed. There was a gag in his mouth and a blindfold over his eyes. He could hear the voices of several women and when they realized that he was awake they told him that he would have to have sex with all of them.

He thinks that four women had sex with him, some of them several times. Whenever he had difficulty maintaining an erection there were threats of castration and a knife was held against his scrotum. The women also stimulated his penis. He was held prisoner for over twenty-four hours; then he was dressed and taken by car to an isolated area where he was released, while still blindfolded with his hands loosely tied. He did not notify the police because he was afraid that his friends would find out and think that he was less than a man because he had been raped by women (Sarrel and Masters).

A thirty-seven-year-old man was accosted late one evening by two women who forced him at gunpoint inside an abandoned building. They made him undress, tied his hands, manipulated him to erection and had intercourse with him a number of times. When he could no longer maintain an erection, they abused his genitals and rectum. When he fainted, they untied his hands and left him.

A twenty-three year old medical student became involved in a sexual bondage session with a woman who tied him to a bed. He panicked and tried to end the game, but the woman became aggressive, demanded intercourse, and threatened him with a scalpel if he did not perform. Although frightened he was able to respond sexually (Murray).

WOMEN "RAPING" WOMEN

Women who are sexually assaulted by other women rarely report the offense. Such sexual assaults may involve one lesbian assaulting another lesbian, a lesbian and a nonlesbian victim, lesbians posing as men and seducing naive young girls below the age of consent, female gang initiation rites, and a husband-wife team.

Lesbians Sexually Assaulting Lesbian Lovers

Some of these sexual assaults are like marital rape. During an ongoing lesbian relationship one lover insists on sex at a time when her partner does not want it and refuses to give her consent. A sexual assault may also occur when one of the lovers wishes to punish her partner for suspected or actual infidelity, for wanting to terminate the relationship, or for other reasons. Punishment includes sexual assault as in the following case.

A young woman, who said that she had "raped" ten women, described her usual sexual relationships with other women as "Oral sex, finger fuck, kisses and bites all over the body, just nicks." When asked to explain what she meant by rape, she replied "Fist fuck them, make them bleed." She described some of the assaults:

"I always do violence when my lovers leave. I've tied many women to the bed, to cut them, beat them up, or fist fuck them. One girl told me I cut her bad, she asked a girl friend to drive her to the hospital. She told me I made her beg me to make love to her. If she hadn't convinced me to make love to her, I would have killed her".

"I raped her once and almost killed her once by choking her; she was blue. I was going to cut her up, but the cops came."

"One woman—I broke in her home, I held a butcher knife over her head and told her 'Doesn't it frighten you?' I raped her, I cut her. I told her if she said anything to the cops, I'd get out eventually, I'd kill her."

"I beat her up . . . her chest was laid right open all across, she got cut the worst. She has bad scars where I cut her".

"I beat her up a lot if she didn't do what I wanted her to do, and I cut her, just small cuts. She said I choked her, that's why she moved."

"I punched her, hit her, pulled a knife on her; I was drunk. I woke up the next morning and her leg was all out of shape. I broke her ankle in five places. She told the doctor she slipped on ice."

"I fisted her and made her bleed."

One of her lovers wanted to renew relations with her even after she had been tied up and cut over her chest with a knife. The young woman, who sexually and brutally assaulted her lovers, had been sexually assaulted as a child.

Lesbian Assaults in Jails

A lesbian confined in jail without access to another lesbian may assault a nonlesbian prisoner. There is an attempt at seduction, but when that fails, there is use of force. A female prisoner reported that she had been raped in the middle of the night by her cellmate. "She grabbed me in a position where I couldn't move and started kissing my neck and sucking on my breasts and things like that down my stomach, and began licking and sucking my pubic hair. She lay on top of me, pinning my arms by crossing one wrist over the other, and grinding on me until she had an orgasm. She put her tongue and fingers in my vagina."

Lesbians Posing as Men Seduce Young Girls

A lesbian of masculine appearance, holds a man's job, uses a man's name, cuts her hair short, cross-dresses as a male, and in the community is believed to be a man. She seduces a young woman who thinks that she has had sexual relations with a man. She has been deceived by the skilful use of a concealed dildo.

A nineteen-year-old girl, who posed as a man, was arrested and charged with sexual assault and criminal impersonation after three fourteen-year-old girls said they thought they were having sex with a seventeen-year-old boy. One girl said they had sexual relations every other day for over a period of five months. Another girl said they had sex fifteen times and the third girl said twelve times.

The mother of one girl said she had been with the suspect and her daughter many times and never suspected anything. One of the girls when asked if she ever suspected anything, replied that they usually had sex in a darkened room and "he" never removed "his" shirt and always remained under the covers. The nineteen-year-old woman was arrested after making harassing telephone calls to one of the girls who had broken-up with her. When the police arrested her she had a driver's license in a woman's name. She said the license belonged to her sister, but it was a picture of herself.

A HUSBAND–WIFE TEAM

A seventeen-year-old girl, who was drinking and watching pornographic movies with a couple she had met at a party, describes the sexual assault: "Suddenly Bob put handcuffs on my hands and told me we were going downstairs. When I refused, he hit me. He kept telling me to be a good girl and he wouldn't hit me anymore. We got downstairs and he took my clothes off, while the whole time his wife knew and watched what was going on. We were in the basement bedroom and he put the cuffs on behind me, put me on the bed, and sexually assaulted me.

"Then he told me how his wife was a bisexual and liked girls. He told her to take off her clothes and join us, so she did. He told her to suck my breasts and made me do the same to her. Then he told her to suck my vaginal area and me do the same to her. After that, he told me to have oral sex with him, and told his wife to do it after me. Then they were having intercourse and oral sex while I was on the bed and she was leaning on me pinning me down so I couldn't move.

After they were done, he said we were going upstairs. He made his wife walk first with me in the middle, while he was holding on to me and carrying my clothes. We got upstairs and sat down and that's when he threatened me with his knife by putting the sharp edge on my back. After I said I wouldn't tell anyone what happened, he told me he would walk me home. I got my clothes and purse and went to the bathroom where I locked the door and got out through the bathroom window, out the back gate, and ran with one shoe on. I left the other one there.

MEN RAPING MEN

In every wolf is a punk looking for revenge.

Prison saying

Rape of men is a forbidden topic. Women have difficulty reporting rape, men often find it impossible to report that they have been sodomized. The FBI *Uniform Crime Reports* do not provide statistics on sexual assaults of men. Rada, in 1983, reported that in Albuquerque, New Mexico, approximately 8 percent of victims seeking help from the Rape Crisis Center were male. The Sexual Assault Response Team in the same city reported that approximately 10 percent of their victims were male. Ages of victims ranged from five to forty-five years. In San Francisco, which has a large gay population, it has been reported that as many as 50 percent of all rape victims are men.

Men are most likely to be sexually assaulted in prisons. Whenever a bus load of new prisoners arrives at a penitentiary, the wolves are waiting to select suitable young prisoners for seduction or intimidation. Older prisoners may offer friendship, advice, drugs or protection. Direct use of force can be sudden, without warning, brutal and overpowering. The victim is seized when there are no guards within sight or hearing and accomplices stand by to warn of the approach of any staff. Repeated anal and oral sexual assaults by several prisoners are followed by threats of death if the prisoner reports the assaults.

A twenty-two-year-old male prisoner described his rape by another prisoner:

Around 10:30 A.M. I went to see my lawyer about my case. I came back around 11:00 A.M. and then went to lunch. After I came back from lunch and went to my cell, as I was leaving two men came into my cell and asked me who I had snitched on and why. When I said that I had not snitched on anybody, they started to hit me around my head. They stopped the assault about three or four times and asked who I had snitched on and then started hitting and kicking me again. Then they took me from my cell to another cell on another tier.

Another man then entered the cell and said that he should stab me for being a snitch. He threatened that he would stab me if I didn't do what he told me to do. He then told me to take off my clothes and to lay on the bunk on my stomach and keep quiet. He then entered my rectum. Afterwards he told me to take a shower and clean up real good, and said that if I went to the police he would kill me. While this was going on the first two men were standing outside of the cell watching for the guard and also what was happening in the cell. I then wrote a note asking to be moved quickly and gave it to a guard while he was taking count.

This victim took action to protect himself from further rapes, but many prisoners are afraid to do anything and are raped over and over again. These punks, as they are called, are looked down on by the other inmates. The rapists, or wolves, do not see themselves as being homosexual.

Group rapes and use of violence are also a common feature of homosexual rapes outside prison walls. The use of alcohol or drugs by both offender and victim is often a factor. The circumstances of the rape tend to be the same as those encountered by women victims. A hitchhiker is offered a ride and is raped in the back of the car. The victim is seized in the street, dragged behind some bushes and assaulted. The boss after a Christmas party at work attacks a junior male employee. Young men, as well as young women, are very vulnerable while jogging alone in a park.

In the navy, a sailor who is causing trouble for other sailors has to be taught a lesson. While he is sleeping, a blanket is thrown over him so that he cannot see the men who are beating him. Rarely a "blanket party" involves sexual assault by men with different motives.

Anal sex is the usual form of homosexual assault, but the victim may also be forced to suck the offender's penis or to masturbate him. In half of twenty-two cases of male rape reported by Groth and Burgess, the offender made an effort to get his victim to ejaculate either through fellatio or masturbation. These victims were especially concerned about their own sexual arousal, one commenting:

"I always thought a guy couldn't get hard if he was scared, and when this guy took me off it really messed up my mind. I thought maybe something was wrong with me. I didn't know what it meant and this really bothered me."

MEN RAPING THE DEAD

Living women felt nothing but repulsion for me, it was quite natural I should turn to the dead, who have never repulsed me.

Necrophilic grave digger

A man with necrophilic fantasies extolled the virtues of a corpse as a sexual object. He described with relish the feeling of power and security that he could enjoy in making love to a corpse; it is there when wanted, you put it away when finished with it, it makes no demands, it is never frustrating, never unfaithful, never reproachful; persecution and guilt, he said, could be quite done away with. In his sexual relationships with women he demanded immobility and absolute compliance (Segal). A corpse is not going to criticize premature ejaculation, loss of erection, or other sexual failures. There is no risk of pregnancy and no possibility of the victim making a report to the police.

Necrophilic fantasies are acted out by men who ask their sexual partners to pretend that they are dead. They may pay a prostitute to make herself up to look like a corpse, dress in a shroud, then lie in a coffin.

It is not unusual for a rape-murderer to have intercourse with the victim as she is dying or shortly after her death. A few return, hours or even weeks later, to have sex with the corpse. Men who prefer sex with the dead seek employment as hospital orderlies, funeral home employees, mortuary attendants, and grave diggers. Some of them also rape the living, and some rape and kill.

One grave digger disinterred twenty bodies of children for sexual purposes. Another grave digger, who dug up the bodies of young girls, had no sense of smell, which must surely be an advantage for a necrophilic. Some authorities, however, attach significance to the stench as a psychological factor in the genesis of this perversion.

An alert detective investigating fires in two mortuaries noticed the outlines of a man's hands in the soot on the chest of a seventy-four-year-old woman who had been dead for five days. There was sperm in her vagina. The arsonist was suspected of having sex with the body of another elderly woman, and of trying to set fire to the pubic area of one woman. He set eleven other fires. On questioning he said he would read about the fires in the newspapers and he would have a feeling that he had set them.

Sadistic serial arsonists may also commit sex offenses and may have a childhood history of cruelty to animals, fire setting and bed wetting. Some seek employment in fire departments or work involving use of explosives. This man while in the navy received training in fire fighting and in underwater demolition using explosives. He applied to join two fire departments. His pediatrician was surprised that he had hemorrhoids at the age of seven months. Was he sexually assaulted at this age? He received sex instruction from his mother. She said that at three years of age he played with matches.

He was given a sentence of ten to twelve years. Ten years later he was in trouble again for attempts to burn down a neighbor's home while the family was sleeping. Previously he had called to report a fire, and there was increasing excitement in his voice. Another time he commented, "If somebody says the wrong thing I'm burned up and I'm mad." Dogs had disappeared from his neighborhood and it was thought that he had disposed of them.

Cases of homosexual necrophilia have been reported. A twenty-two-year-old married homosexual male had fantasies of a sexual relationship with a male wholly in his power—a man completely drugged or drunk, completely unconscious, a man powerless in the stocks, or, best of all, a man who was dead. While his wife was in the hospital, he took a male friend up into the mountains on a pretext, shot him in the head, indulged in anal intercourse and other sexual activities, then threw his body down a mine shaft. Later he said, "I do not think anything would have stopped me. I was mad with power; I had him in my power and nothing could stop me." He was sentenced to fifty years in prison (Bartholomew et al.).

Dennis Nilsen, the English homosexual murderer, who killed fifteen young men, including homosexuals and male prostitutes, would undress, wash and dry the bodies of his victims, and he either masturbated or had sex between the thighs of six of the victims. He used to put talc on his face and body to look like a corpse, gaze at his body in a mirror, and masturbate.

MEN RAPING ANIMALS

Men rape a variety of animals, but they are seldom arrested or convicted because their victims are incapable of either reporting the crime or giving evidence in court. Radzinowicz, in England, found that only 2 percent of 1,985 sexual offenses involved bestiality. Bluglass, in twenty-one years experience of assessing English offenders, found no more than a dozen cases of bestiality.

The writer, in over in over thirty seven years of examining criminal offenders, encountered only one man who admitted to sex acts with an animal. Gebhard et al., in their study of 1,356 males convicted of sex offenses, found only five cases of men legally punished for sexual behavior with animals.

Occasionally an offender is detected in the act. An elderly couple arriving home saw a man in their back yard copulating with their

Labrador dog. He was kneeling behind the dog and holding the dog by the hips. He looked up but continued for about thirty seconds to what looked like completion. When he was done, he stood up, calmly zipped up his pants, stood for a moment, then walked casually to the back fence. He jumped the fence, got on a bicycle and rode down the alley.

Bestiality is much more common than is suggested by criminal statistics and the personal experience of forensic psychiatrists. The Kinsey report on sexual behavior in the human male indicated that about 17 percent of farm boys have complete sexual relations with animals, and perhaps as many more have relations which are not carried through to climax. It would be a mistake to assume that sex with animals is largely confined to farm boys.

Animal rapists resemble those child molesters who seduce their victims, do things for them, and do not use force. One young man wrote a long statement talking about Susie. He had dated other girls but no one cared for him as much as Susie; she was his true love and he would never leave her for another woman. He mentioned how offended he was when someone suggested he might be interested in a male. Never, he wasn't a fag. Then suddenly you realize he is talking about his mare, that he would never leave her for another mare, and that he would not think of having a relationship with a stallion.

Offenders may come under suspicion by subscribing to animal pornography magazines, by writing or sending computer messages to fellow aficionados, and by taking pictures or videotapes of their sexual acts with animals. There are persons who lead a very active sex life with animals and in their letters they write at length about their experiences:

"I'd even have sex with a Hereford, although I think they're rather homely . . . all the deer species are very sexy . . . I'm basically into acts that animals can enjoy too. Its more of a turn on to see them enjoying it, than if they're not enjoying it . . . I put Karo on my dick when I'm first starting a mare into fellating me, so it tastes good to her and she likes to have it in her mouth. I don't believe in hurting animals . . . You are right about range cattle, they are very wild and not near as good . . . I fell in love with the horse I bought, I had oral sex the first day I got her, and had intercourse with her about a month later."

This extract from an animal lover's letter to a friend is revealing:

> I also spoke to my other California friend last night, and he tells me that he has five stallions in his barn, now, along with mares and fillies, and they are all cooperative. I know from personal experience that his mares sure are good.

Zowie, I do like mares. I have also visited the dairy farm, three times in the past week and had success each time! Including a two hour session with an almost jet black cow! She had a white udder, and one white spot on her hip . . . What a fuck! I sure needed it. I just went out and enjoyed my favorite mare, I was so wound up thinking about that cow . . . She was great, as usual.

My friend with the stallions says he will contact you as soon as I see something of you in action with a horse. I know you are shy, and also getting the video is difficult, but, it will be kept among true animal lovers. Oh yes, I have some more good stuff with deer, including a buck deer, and a llama!, along with mares and a cow. And a stallion. Ain't I a tease! I really want to see your stuff. Oh lord, the TV is on behind me, and some of the commercials for women's cunt rags and wash are getting so gross, and blatant they are disgusting. Now its "After period, when you need a douche the most". UGH!!! Oh well, I have to go work on my horse trailer's brakes, so I will bid you adieu.

REFERENCES

Bartholomew, A.A., Milte, K.L., and Galkbaly, Frank.: Homosexual necrophilia. *Med Sci Law, 18:*29, 1978.

Bluglass, Robert. Bestiality. In Bluglass, Robert and Bowden, Paul. (Ed.) *Principles and Practice of Forensic Psychiatry.* New York, Churchill Livingstone, 1990.

Federal Bureau of Investigation: *Uniform Crime Reports for the United States 1993.* Washington, U.S. Government Printing Office, 1994.

Ferdinand, T. N.: The criminal patterns of Boston since 1849. *Amer J Sociol, 73:*84, 1967.

Gebhard, P., et al.: *Sex Offenders.* New York, Harper Row and Paul Hober, 1965.

Groth, A.N., and Burgess, A.W.: Male rape: Offenders and victims. *Amer J Psychiat, 137:*806, 1980.

Kinsey, A.C., Pomeroy, W.B., and Martin, C.E.: *Sexual Behavior in the Human Male.* Philadelphia, W.B. Saunders, 1948.

Kourany, R.F.C., Hill, R.Y., and Hollender, M.H.: The age of sexual consent. *Bull Am Acad Psychiatry Law 14:*171, 1986.

Malinowski, B.: *The Sexual Life of Savages in Northwestern Melanesia.* New York, Eugenics, 1929.

Murray, Linda.: When men are raped by women. *Sexual Medicine Today* July, 1982.

Rada, R.T.: *Clinical Aspects of the Rapist.* New York, Grune & Stratton 1978.

Radzinowicz, L.: *Sexual Offenses.* London, Macmillan, 1957.

Reaves, B.A.: Using NIBRS data to analyze violent crime. *Bureau of Justice Statistics Technical Report* October, 1993.

Sarrel P. M., and Masters, W. H.: Sexual molestation of men by women. *Arch Sex Behav, 11:*117, 1982.

Segal, H. A necrophilic phantasy. *Int J Psychoanal, 34:*98, 1953.

Chapter 2

WHY MEN RAPE

THE EXPERTS DISAGREE

A man in passion rides a horse that runs away from him.
C.H. Spurgeon, *Ploughman's Pictures.*

Rape is not a crime of irrational, impulsive, uncontrollable lust, but is a deliberate, hostile, violent act of degradation.

Susan Brownmiller, *Against Our Will.*

The explanation of rape is usually sought in the obvious conscious motivation of sexual desire, perhaps associated with other motives as envy, revenge, anger, power, and sadism. Often indeed there is clear evidence of such factors, but even when they are present they do not always provide an adequate explanation for the crime. The offender himself may seek to explain his conduct in like manner. Yet the mainsprings of human conduct are so complex as to cast doubt on such simple solutions.

The conscious confessions of criminals and a statement of the circumstances of the crime, be it ever so complete, will never sufficiently explain why the individual in the given circumstances had to commit just that act. External circumstances very often do not motivate the deed at all, and the doer, did he wish to be frank, would mostly have to acknowledge that he really did not himself exactly know what impelled him to do it; most often, however, he is not so frank, not even to himself, but subsequently looks for and finds explanation of his conduct, which was in many ways incomprehensible, and psychically only imperfectly motivated, that is to say, he rationalizes something irrational (Ferenczi).

A SERIAL RAPE OFFENDER WHO KILLED

For example, a young man who was arrested after he had made several homicidal assaults on women was quick to agree with the district attorney that his assaults were for the purpose of sexual gratification. At first sight this explanation appears satisfactory. After rendering his victims unconscious he would proceed to rape them. But surely sexual intercourse can be achieved at less cost. The man was of pleasing appearance and experienced little difficulty in establishing social relations with members of the opposite sex. He lived in a large city where it was relatively easy to make the acquaintance of prostitutes. Furthermore, intercourse with an unconscious woman in a dark alley with the ever-present risk of detection can scarcely be pleasurable.

Not all his victims were rendered unconscious. He would pick up a young girl at a drive-in or on the city streets and drive to a lover's lane. On arrival, without any attempt at seduction, he would tell the girl to remove her underclothing. Removing a large hunting knife from the glove compartment he would ostentatiously clean his fingernails while commenting on the dangers of physical resistance. In these circumstances one would not expect to find a loving embrace. On psychiatric examination I pointed out to the young man that he must harbour considerable feelings of hostility toward the opposite sex.

When he rejected this suggestion, I reminded him that he had fractured the skulls of two women, attacked others with a hatchet and in other ways physically assaulted a number of women. Grudgingly he agreed that perhaps he had acted in a hostile manner toward a number of women. He acknowledged that the fleeting tense moments with his victims were not the most appropriate circumstances for sexual union. I then asked if any woman had made sexual advances to him. There was indeed one such instance, an attractive young woman who, while on a date made it clear that she was willing to have sexual relations with him. He added rather primly that this suggestion upset him and he drove her straight back to her home.

After further discussion he began to realize that sexual gratification was not the explanation for his assaults on women. He requested psychiatric treatment for which he was eligible under a sexual psychopath law. I pointed out that treatment would mean exploration of the source of his hostility to women, and that this hostility probably originated in his childhood. As the only significant members of the opposite sex in his early life were his mother and his grandmother attention would be focused upon them. At this he became extremely angry and flexing his biceps, shouted out that he would bust the teeth out of any blankety blank psychiatrist who suggested that his mother had anything to do with his problem.

As this was precisely what I was doing I thought it wise to change the subject. His extreme reaction brought to mind Shakespeare's comment, "The lady doth protest too much, me thinks." When his anger subsided he became very anxious and volunteered that he had committed a number of assaults which the police did not know about; stating "I'm cutting my throat by doing this" he gave time, place and circumstance of these earlier crimes. He knew that I would report this information to the court as I had previously told him that the examination was not confidential.

Although he claimed that his relationship with his mother was a good one and that she disapproved of his wayward behavior, it was significant from his account that she had in the past shielded him from the police and hence from detection and that she gave tacit approval for his delinquent behavior. When she visited him on the ward she would sit close to him in a conspiratory manner and the pair would stop talking whenever a nurse approached within earshot. On one occasion, however, the two were overheard reviewing with obvious pleasure one of his earlier offenses. His mother in her childhood had been placed in a home for delinquents, and had later been acquitted on the charge of murdering her husband.

This youth was committed to the state hospital for treatment. One time his mother was driving him away from the hospital on leave and the sun was in her eyes, so she pulled down the sun visor. When she did this a packet of contraceptives fell in her lap. She commented what a fool her other son was to use contraceptives as they took a lot of pleasure out of sex. Surely an inappropriate comment in the circumstances. The son later revealed that he used to bring a stripper home in the hope that his mother would tell him not to do this, but she never did.

At the age of thirty-two after a period of confinement in the state penitentiary he was released. Within two months he decided to ask me to treat him and, unknown to me, he was within ten feet of me outside the University Hospital when he realized it was too late, for he had already killed a woman. Within a year of his release from the penitentiary, he raped a number of women and stabbed four of them. He was suspected of killing two women and he pleaded guilty to one murder. Alongside the body of the victim outside a church, the words, "I hate women" were written in the snow.

Originally he did not reveal his great feelings of anger at his grandmother, who was given responsibility for his care after the birth of a younger brother when he was thirteen months of age. "I was given away by my mother and shunned by my grandmother, a cold blonde bitch on wheels, a cold unloving monster. My feelings about my mother are just as screwed up. I had this sense of worthlessness, of being not loved, of being a little monster. Every time I suffer, I'm made to suffer, it's a woman that does it, and I suffer without the possibility of forgiveness. Somewhere in the back of my mind I've got the impression even this institution is a woman." He was referring to the state penitentiary where he was serving a life sentence.

He had a long history of sex offenses. At the age of ten he started window peeping and stealing women's underclothing from clothes lines. In addition to cutting up some of the underclothing, he cut up pictures of well-dressed women—symbolic murder. He also dressed in women's clothing. There was no indecent exposure and no preoccupation with pornography. For a brief period, when he was much older, he made obscene telephone calls to shock women.

At twelve, he started assaulting women, then quickly grabbing their breasts and buttocks. He had no feelings of sexual arousal but was gratified by the frightened screams of his victims. Later he started raping his victims. Once again the assaults were brief and violent. He never tied up any of his victims, although he thought of it and carried adhesive tape, rope, and baling wire. The sex was seldom pleasurable. Sometimes he was unable to get an erection, sometimes there was premature ejaculation, and sometimes there was a "reasonable simulation of sex."

Most of his victims resembled his grandmother, "tall, bitchy blondes"; some resembled his mother, dark haired and, as he would like to think of her, well-dressed. He liked to look at blondes, but he would not look at dark haired women "in a sexual way."

Although he pleaded guilty to one murder, he revealed later that he had killed two women and had tried very hard to kill two others. The only reason he didn't kill the other two was because he was interrupted in the act. He did not consciously plan to kill his rape victims but acknowledged that he killed or attempted to kill them because they could identify him from police department mug shots of him.

Later he would have fantasies about the sexual assaults and would convince himself that the woman was a compliant victim. She was willing to have sex but did not want it. These fantasies did not center on the killing. "Violence was the only way to get what I wanted, I never set out to do it . . . there is a side of me that is sadistic."

Between eleven and thirteen he was cruel to animals. He would put turpentine on the rear ends of dogs and cats. With the use of bird seed and a bird trap he captured birds, which he killed with explosives. After putting a two inch firecracker down the bird's throat he would release it. The bird would fly about fifteen feet then "bang."

This man's hatred of women clearly was a major factor in his rapes, his brutal physical assaults, and ultimately his murder of women. He felt that his mother rejected him "physically" by asking his grandmother to care for him after his brother's birth, and that his grandmother rejected him emotionally. His anger toward them was displaced on to other women.

Anger alone did not fully explain his rapes. As a school student he was aware that his mother did not set limits on sexual behavior that other mothers would have discouraged. Indeed, she encouraged such behavior, for example, by showing pleasure when he told her about his rapes. His father, who died when he was sixteen, did not seem to play a major role in his life. He described him as a nebulous puff of smoke.

A SERIAL RAPE OFFENDER WHO SHOT A VICTIM

One afternoon a man with a stocking mask on his face entered the home of a young married woman with the intention of raping her. The woman was forced to undress, but she succeeded in distracting his attention for a moment and while she was running from the house in the nude, he shot her. The bullet went in her back and came out her chest. She stumbled ten feet and fell in the snow. When she looked up, she saw him pointing the gun at her and she thought he was going to kill her. She pleaded with him and he left.

The thirty-one-year-old offender had served time for burglary and for taking indecent liberties with a five-year-old girl (taking her pants down and touching her). He told me that he had committed fifteen rapes or attempted rapes, over one hundred acts of indecent exposure, fifty to sixty burglaries mainly to get women's underclothing, several armed robberies, auto theft and repeated acts of arson including the destruction of a warehouse and a garage.

He specialized in the armed robbery of beauty shops and wig shops. Most armed robbers leave as quickly as possible after they get the money, but this man also had sex in mind. Wearing his stocking mask and armed with a gun, he robbed about eight women in one Denver shop, then told them to go in the back room and made them undress. Before leaving he raped two of the women in front of the other victims.

He did not realize the size of a beauty shop in Cheyenne, Wyoming and when he found at least twenty women inside, he just made them lie down on the floor and took their money. He left without committing the rape he had planned.

After shooting the victim in the attempted rape, he was driving out of the area when he saw a five- or six-year-old girl. He wanted to touch her and expose himself to her, but by the time he parked his car she had disappeared. In a nearby town, he put on his stocking mask, and went into a beauty shop. He ordered the three women in the shop to undress and told two of them to perform sex acts with each other. After raping one woman he tied her up, forced her and the other women into the bathroom, and returned to Denver. A few days later he was arrested and charged with assault to commit murder.

The Offender Looks at Himself

My mother didn't think I could do anything wrong. She overprotected me, wouldn't let me play ball, wouldn't even let me ride a bicycle. She even wanted me to stay inside. She taught me embroidery, stuff like that, cooking, trying to make a real sissy out of me. She dressed me in baby dresses for quite a while. She got dolls for me. She told me I played with them for quite a while.

This overprotectiveness, my mother would do things to humiliate me, spit on her handkerchief, clean my face in a bus, in church, in front of other people. I'd feel downright humiliated. To this day I don't know how to tie a necktie, she always done this. I used to sleep in her room. My stepfather slept in another room. When I was eleven or twelve, I saw her naked a few times. It didn't embarrass her. She was always trying to hug me when I was younger. Thirteen or fourteen on I wouldn't like to kiss her. When I went to the navy, I felt embarrassed just hugging her. I knew she wanted to kiss me goodbye. I wanted her to do it on the cheek, she did it on the lips.

My father died when I was about five and I don't remember too much about him. My mother remarried when I was seven but he died within about a year. She married again. He used to whip me. He'd threaten to kill me, he'd threaten to kill somebody as a matter of speech. He threatened to kill my brother-in-law when I was fifteen and I took the gun from him. I always had a fear of him.

Around eleven or twelve, if I was masturbating, I'd use a picture from a catalogue, but I'd get visions of my mother naked and I'd feel guilty. I'd try to get rid of that vision of her and finish masturbating. As long as I had that vision of her I couldn't masturbate and that's still the same way today. When I was fourteen or fifteen, I had these fantasies my mother would be sitting in a chair with nothing on but a garter belt and stockings and would have her legs spread. When I had these fantasies it was sickening.

At thirteen, my "mother" told me I was adopted; I felt I didn't belong to the family . . . I felt like a stray dog somebody would pick up. I don't feel like anything, just a piece of garbage. I used to have daydreams of finding out who my mother was, where she lived, knock on the door. When she answered it, I'd tell her who I was, stick the revolver right in her gut and just shoot her dead. Hell, she threw me away.

My problem with women must have started around thirteen or fourteen. The first thing I ever done was to a woman walking down the street. I felt underneath her dress between her legs. Then I ran off. I done that quite a few times. Then I started exposing myself. I've been chased for that and for peeping Tom. My first attempted rape, I was about twenty-four, the girl was pretty nice. I doubled up my fist and hit her in the face as hard as I could. She just stood there screaming. It scared me off. Then there was a twelve-year-old girl. I couldn't get in her. The next time I used a gun.

When this urge—indecent exposure, burglary, rape—hits me, I have an urge to have a bowel motion. Often in a burglary I stop and have a bowel motion. I had a bowel motion once with my clothes on, I couldn't hold it. It happened just as I stepped out of the house.

My second wife divorced me while I was in the penitentiary. It really hurt me; I had fantasies of killing her. She was a beautician and after I left the pen I rang up a whole bunch of beauty shops to find her. I wonder if that doesn't mean something, the places I held up were beauty shops. I was serious about wanting to kill her. It was the only time I had sadistic fantasies, tying her down over an ant pile, keeping her alive a long time, cut her eyelids off so she couldn't close her eyes, keeping her alive and torturing her.

Comment

This man had sadistic fantasies of stabbing a woman in the stomach with a butcher knife, then having intercourse in the wound; fantasies of shooting people while driving down the highway; and fantasies of blowing up trains and highway bridges. He was a firesetter as a child and as an adult. A lot of times he would set little fires and these fires would give him an erection. Bed wetting was a problem, but there was no history of cruelty to animals. A stepfather used to whip and threaten to kill him. His seductive, adoptive mother tried to bring him up as a girl and there were times he wished he was a woman. He daydreamed that he was a lesbian making love to another woman and he had numerous pictures of lesbians at play.

A THIRD SERIAL RAPE OFFENDER

Unlike the two previous serial rape offenders, this man did not shoot or kill any of his victims. His first arrest was at the age of twelve for theft. Then there were convictions on charges of burglary, robbery, theft, rape, criminal trespassing, and escape. At twenty, while attending law enforcement classes at a college in Greeley, over fifty miles from Denver, he was arrested on two charges of criminal trespass after he was detected in two apartments. The first time he said he was looking for an apartment to rent, but a sign in front of the building said "For Women Only." The second time he said he was looking for work.

While awaiting trial in Greeley, he was released on bond and six days later a woman was raped in her apartment in the Capitol Hill area of Denver. In the next three months, seven other women in the Capitol Hill area became victims of similar burglary-rapes. The victims were all single white women living in apartments in the same neighborhood. Vaginal rape was from the rear, as was anal rape of five of the victims. The suspect would grab victims, choke them, prevent them from looking at him, threaten to kill them, take their bank cards and demand the secret number.

This rapist was not identified by the police in Denver, but these pattern rapes stopped after the judge in Greeley sentenced the subject of this report to two and a half years in prison for criminal trespass. Almost two years later, at the age of twenty-three, he was released from custody. Two days later he started pawning small items in Denver area pawn shops. The Capitol Hill rapist was back in business, criminal business.

This was his pattern of rape. Stalking women, peeping into their rooms, then breaking into their apartments, usually taking small items and pawning them. Some victims noticed that items were missing, but many thought the items had been misplaced and did not think they had been stolen. One victim did not report to the police the loss of hundreds of dollars from a desk drawer and a purse. Later, the burglar returned to their apartments and raped them.

Although he did not injure his victims, he terrorized them and was clearly a sadistic rapist, very much concerned with his power and control. By day or night he seized victims around the neck while they were answering the front door, walking from one room to another, stepping out of a shower, or sleeping in bed. Then quickly, he covered their eyes so they could not see him, threatened to kill them and warned them not to scream. "If you scream, I'll kill you; If you move, I'll kill you; If you look at me, I'll kill you; I should kill you now; You're not cooperating, I'm really going to have to kill you." Over and over again, he would repeat these threats.

A victim told police: "I noticed that the door was ajar, but I didn't think anything of it since I'm usually but not always careful to shut it completely. I opened the door and he pushed me down. I really didn't see him. He pushed me down to the floor with his hands around my neck from behind me. He said 'If you scream, I'll kill you'. I think I screamed when he got me at first. He was squeezing my neck, like strangling me. He said 'You shouldn't leave your door unlocked'. He asked, 'Is there anyone else in the house?' After I said no, he repeated 'Are you sure there's no one else in the house?' I remember him covering my eyes and that he said, 'If you look at me I'll kill you'."

He was usually armed with a knife, sometimes taken from a kitchen drawer, but he told some victims that he had a gun. He would take his time running the sharp edge of his knife down the victim's back. He traced intricate designs on the lower back near the genital region of two victims, further terrorizing them. Usually there was both anal and vaginal rape from behind while the victim was lying face down.

The sexual assault was brief, sometimes as short as one to three minutes, and always he insisted that the victim take a shower. Although the rape was brief he would spend from one to three hours in the apartment. He would walk the victim through each room in her apartment. There were long discussions that highlighted two subjects: his boasting and his control over his victim. He would claim that he was a big drug dealer and that the police as well as high level rival drug dealers were searching for him. The dealers wanted to kill him.

He would question the victim extensively about her personal life, including her name, her car, her work address, and telephone number. Before leaving he would disable the telephone and search the apartment for ATM (automated teller machine) cards, department store credit cards, and for small items of value. He would demand to know the secret number for the ATM cards and warned that if given the wrong number he would come back and kill the woman. After leaving he would go to a nearby ATM card machine and withdraw money.

A woman thought she heard some one in her apartment late at night. She got out of bed and saw a tall muscular black man about six feet two inches standing in the doorway of her kitchen. He clamped a hand over her mouth and told her to shut up, that he wasn't a burglar and didn't want to rape her. He said he was running from some people and needed to hide.

With one hand around her neck he choked her several times until she promised to keep quiet. With one hand still around her neck, and with one hand clamped on her left arm, he took her to her bedroom to turn out the light, to the back door to make sure that it was locked, to the front door and back to the bedroom. He began asking her personal questions, such as her name, what she did for a living, and her sign of the Zodiac.

He said he was a drug dealer and that he had made enough money in the drug trade to own a $285,000 home and a Mercedes car. He said the guy he was running from had ten or twelve street guys out looking for him because he had taken money or owed money to the guy. He said he had been shot at and he was scared. At intervals he reminded her that he would kill her if she made any noise, that he wouldn't leave any fingerprints because he was wearing gloves, that her life wouldn't mean shit because he was running for his own life and he would do anything for his own safety.

After about half an hour he began stroking her back and squeezing her legs. He told her to take off her clothes because she couldn't run if she was naked. Then he tightened his hold on her throat, and said he had killed a woman before and wouldn't hesitate to do it again. When he said he was going to fuck her, she asked him why and he replied that it was just her pussy and he was going to show her how unimportant it was. After raping her, he apologized saying he could justify everything up to this point but not the rape.

He said he was scared and ashamed, that he wanted to make sure that she got counselling and that he would send a dozen roses to apologize. He claimed to be a Vietnam vet and said he had seen men (soldiers) rape innocent women and children, but he had been a good soldier and had never participated in gang rapes, so he couldn't believe what he had just done. He asked her if she was religious and would she go to church with him.

In his last rape in Denver, the victim fought him, scratched his face, grabbed his testicles, and attempted to escape. He choked her to the point of unconsciousness three times and beat her severely. After raping her he tied her hands and wrists together behind her back with electrical cord. This was the only rape victim that resisted him and the only one that he beat severely and choked to the point of unconsciousness.

There was the usual demand for the secret number on her bank card, the threat to kill if she gave the wrong number and the warning, over and over again, "If you scream, I'll kill you." After he left, she was able to get the cord off her wrists and call the police. She remembered that about a year earlier she had seen him walk through her back yard. He came very close to her, asked her how she was doing, and then left through the backyard gate. About that time there had been several window peeping and prowler incidents involving a tall black man wearing a blue baseball cap.

His distinctive M.O. or method of operation was his undoing. Detectives reviewed the criminal records of all black sex offenders arrested in Denver during the previous five years. Sex offenders in prison or otherwise out of Denver at the times of any of these rapes were eliminated. This time-consuming task pointed to only one offender with a similar M.O. In his parked car, detectives saw a baseball cap with the inscription "You piss me off." A videotape recording at a bank ATM machine shortly after one of his rapes showed a black male wearing a baseball cap with the same inscription withdrawing cash on one of his victim's credit cards.

When detectives went to his mother's home, his brother threatened them and demanded that they leave immediately. His mother told him to go downstairs. Meekly, without hesitation, without a word, he left the room. His mother was clearly in charge in this home. The son, who raped women, was clearly in charge in the homes of his victims. All were young professional women, including two lawyers, a graphics designer, and a therapist. He spent hours exercising control over them and only minutes raping them. Control and power were more important to him than sex, but his rapes were the ultimate expression of his power and control.

A search of his home revealed items belonging to his rape victims. When he realized the police were looking for him he travelled to Dallas, Montreal, New York City, and Miami. FBI agents in a nation-wide manhunt traced him to a wholesale plumbing company in Atlanta, Georgia. When arrested he told FBI agents that he wanted to kill the woman who identified his photograph in a lineup. "I could have shot her in the face; she ruined my life." It was estimated that during his criminal career, he had raped over forty women.

When he went on trial he made every effort to remain in control over his victims and over the court. He insisted on defending himself and filed endless motions, making all kinds of demands. Constantly he ignored the orders of the judge, for example, by continuing to question witnesses on matters that had been ruled inadmissible by the court. Despite objections of the prosecution and repeated admonitions by the court he went his own way.

A judge can control an attorney, if necessary by threatening contempt of court and a brief jail sentence, but such measures mean nothing to a suspect facing a long prison sentence.

During his cross-examination of a detective regarding physical evidence recovered from his car, witnesses observed him handling a piece of physical evidence in a manner that appeared calculated to destroy a highly distinctive and incriminating feature. Eventually the court declared a mistrial.

At both his first and second trials he badgered the women he had raped. While cross-examining a victim, he would stand in front of her holding the very knife he had used at the rape and ask her: "Describe the knife that was used? Is this the knife? How do you know it is the knife?" Whenever a victim replied to one of his questions by saying "You did . . . or you said . . . ". He would request the judge to tell the witness not to say "You" because it had not been proved in court that he committed the rapes. The judge refused this request. At the age of twenty-seven he was sentenced to 376 years in one court and to 24 years in another court. He will probably attempt to escape before he completes his life sentence.

Comment

The first man raped and murdered, the second man raped and shot one of his victims. Both men committed many other sexual offenses. The second man was also involved in arson, armed robberies, and burglaries. Perceptive readers will draw their own conclusions regarding the origins of rape in these two men. Little is known about the childhood background of the third offender. One observer thought that he was effeminate.

These three men are dangerous, sadistic, serial rapists. Sadists are said to account for only a small percentage of all rape offenders. I disagree. In my opinion sadistic rapists are commonly encountered. In their first few rapes, while they still lack confidence, they may not reveal their sadistic nature. Later, most of them confine themselves to terrorizing victims through threats and minimum resort to violence. The third offender who had been raping for many years did not resort to great physical violence until a victim fought him. A few sadistic rapists soon escalate from threats to beatings, torture, and sometimes murder. Sadists are not always sadistic.

SEXUAL SADISM

Just as some pedophiles may never sexually assault children, some sadists may never commit a sadistic crime. This is recognized in the diagnostic criteria for sexual sadism provided in the *Diagnostic and Statistical Manual of Mental Disorders* (DSM–IV) of the American Psychiatric Association:

"A. Over a period of at least six months, recurrent intense sexually arousing fantasies, sexual urges or behaviors involving acts (real, not simulated) in which the psychological or physical suffering (including humiliation) of the victim is sexually exciting to the person.

B. The fantasies, sexual urges, or behaviors cause clinically significant distress or impairment in social, occupational, or other important areas of functioning."

The sadist may confine himself to fantasy. He thinks about what he would like to do to some terrified victim, becomes sexually excited, and masturbates. Perhaps he collects detective magazines with covers showing fearful, bound and gagged rape victims (pornography for the sexual sadist), or he may draw pictures of executions, torture scenes, rapes, and murders.

One man photographed his collection of lifelike female child dolls with breasts, underclothing, and dresses. Some were hanging by the neck from branches of trees with their underclothing pulled aside and the breasts exposed. One doll was naked from the waist down with a fake bomb in the vaginal area. Another doll was wearing an expensive white wedding dress and judging by red splatter on the dress, she had been shot in the heart. Other dolls were lying on the ground with their legs spread apart and the dress pulled up as if they had been raped. Other men slash, burn, mutilate or decapitate dolls, mannequins, or pictures of women.

Some sexual sadists simulate sadistic acts with the aid of a willing girl friend, wife, or prostitute who agrees to a little squeezing, choking, binding, whipping, anal sex, oral sex, vaginal sex, and insertion of foreign objects as a part of the sexual relationship.

A man who solicited a prostitute for bondage undressed her, taped her mouth, handcuffed her hands behind her back, placed her feet inside a pillowcase and taped it to her legs. After inserting a dildo in her vagina, he lay on top of her fully clothed, pinched her nostrils shut and choked her until she lost consciousness. Shortly thereafter, he removed the handcuffs and tape, paid her, and released her.

The prostitute, who took rather a dim view of what he did to her, told police that he was dry humping her because he did not want to risk getting AIDS. When she regained consciousness, he was saying "Hey, hey, wake up." Two days later she still had the marks of the handcuffs on her wrists. He told police that he climaxed and that he might have accidentally put his hand over her nose, cutting off her air. A married man and a member of MENSA, he admitted to using tape and cord to bind four or five other prostitutes during the past three years. He was charged with the misdemeanor offenses of soliciting a prostitute and reckless endangerment.

There is always the risk that the man may get a little too excited and severely beat or strangle his partner. He has broken his agreement with his masochistic or insecure girlfriend or wife and has become a criminal sexual sadist. His business relationship with a prostitute has ended in her serious injury or death, an occupational hazard not covered by worker's compensation.

SADISTIC RAPISTS

Fantasy may satisfy the sexual sadist, but it may also be the first step in his criminal career. Police, on searching the home of a suspected rape-murderer, may find the fantasy material, whether detective magazine covers, drawings, or photographic slides, that show the very murder that had been acted out at the crime scene.

Hazelwood, Dietz, and Warren describe a sadist who apparently acted-out his fantasies on both himself and others. "One offender, who is believed to have kidnapped, tortured, and murdered more than twenty women and young girls, wrote extensively about his sexually sadistic fantasies involving women. These writings included descriptions of his victims' capture, torment, and death by hanging. At the time of his arrest, photographs were found depicting the subject in female attire and participating in autoerotic asphyxia."

These three experts studied thirty male, sexually sadistic criminals, twenty-two of whom were responsible for at least 187 murders. These experts define sexual sadism as a persistent pattern of becoming sexually excited in response to another's suffering. They emphasize that it is the suffering of the victim, not the infliction of physical or psychological pain, that is sexually arousing. In support of their viewpoint, they quote the writings of two unnamed sexual sadists.

"One writes: ' . . . the most important radical aim is to make her suffer since there is no greater power over another person than that of inflicting pain on her to force her to undergo suffering without her being able to defend herself. The pleasure in the complete domination over another person is the very essence of the sadistic drive.'

"Of his sexually sadistic activities with a victim he killed, another offender writes: ' . . . she was writhering(sic) in pain and I loved it. I was now combining my sexual high of rape and my power high of fear to make a total sum that is now beyond explaining . . . I was alive for the sole purpose of causing pain and receiving sexual gratification . . . I was relishing the pain just as much as the sex'.

"Each offender's account confirms that it is the suffering of the victim, not the infliction of physical or psychological pain, that is sexually arousing. In fact, one of these men resuscitated his victim from unconsciousness so that he could continue to savor her suffering. Inflicting pain is a means to create suffering and to elicit the desired responses of obedience, submission, humiliation, fear and terror . . .

"Each of the thirty sexual sadists studied intentionally tortured their victims. Their methods of physical torture included the use of such instruments as hammers, pliers, and electrical cattle prods, and such actions as biting, whipping, burning, insertion of foreign objects into the rectum or vagina, bondage, amputation, asphyxiation to the point of unconsciousness, and insertion of glass rods in the male urethra, to name a few . . .

"The thirty sexual sadists studied also inflicted psychological suffering on their victims. Binding, blindfolding, gagging and holding a victim captive all produce psychological suffering, even if not physically painful. Other psychological tactics used included threats or other forms of verbal abuse, forcing the victim to beg, plead or describe sexual acts, telling the victim in precise detail what was intended, having the victim choose between slavery or death, and offering the victim a choice of means by which to die."

These experts provide additional information on the thirty male sexually sadistic criminals. "Sexual deviations are often associated with other sexual abnormalities, and our study confirmed this for sexual sadism. Forty-three percent of the men participated in homosexual activity as adults, 20 percent engaged in cross-dressing, and 20 percent committed other sexual offenses such as peeping, obscene phone calls, and indecent exposure.

"*Case:* As a teenager, one sexual sadist peeped throughout his neighborhood, masturbating as he watched women undress or have sex. At home, he masturbated repeatedly to fantasies in which he incorporated what he had seen while peeping. As a young adult, he made obscene telephone calls, which lead to his first arrest when he agreed to meet a victim who informed the police. He later exposed himself to a series of victims, which he eventually explained was for the purpose of eliciting their 'shock and fear.'

"He followed women home from shopping malls, determined how much cover was available for peeping and entering the residence, and eventually raped a series of women. In his early rapes, he depended on weapons of opportunity, but later, carried with him a rape kit, which consisted of adhesive tape, handcuffs, precut lengths of rope, and a .45

caliber pistol. He became progressively violent in his sexual assaults, torturing his victims by beating, burning, and pulling their breasts.

"His violence escalated to the point that he so severely pummeled one victim that she lost both breasts. He forcibly raped more than fifty women and was contemplating murder when he was finally apprehended . . .

"Almost invariably, the victims were taken to a location selected in advance that offered solitude and safety for the sadist and little opportunity of escape or rescue for the victim. Such locations included the offender's residence, isolated forests, and even elaborately constructed facilities designed for captivity."

"*Case:* A white male entered a respected modelling agency and advised that he was filming a documentary on drug abuse among preadolescents. He made arrangements to hire two young girls from the agency, and two elderly matrons accompanied them as chaperons. He drove them to his trailer and, at gunpoint, bound the women and placed the girls in a plywood cell he constructed in the trailer. The cell contained beds and additional mattresses for soundproofing. He murdered both women, placing their bodies in garbage bags. He terrorized the girls for more than two days before they were rescued.

"Twenty-three (77%) of the offenders used sexual bondage on their victims, often tying them with elaborate and excessive materials, using neat and symmetrical bindings, and restraining them in a variety of positions. Eighteen (60%) held their victims in captivity for more than twenty-four hours.

"The most common sexual activity was anal rape (22 offenders), followed in frequency by forced fellatio, vaginal rape, and foreign object penetration. Two-thirds of the men subjected their victims to at least three of these four acts . . .

"Eighty-three percent of the victims were strangers to the offender. While the majority of the men selected female victims, one-fourth attacked males exclusively. Sixteen percent of the men assaulted child victims only, and 26 percent attacked both children and adults" (Hazelwood, Dietz and Warren).

SADISM, SEX, AND FIRE

Lust is but a bloody fire,
Kindled with unchaste desire.

Shakespeare, *The Merry Wives of Windsor*

The relationship between sex and fire is illustrated by expressions such as: "You light my fire baby, burning desire, burning kisses, flames of passion, hot pants, to have the hots for someone, and firemen are always in heat." Fire also symbolizes anger as shown by expressions such as: "Fiery look, red with anger, in the heat of anger, to blaze up, fire eater, fire and fury." Anger is another feature of rape.

Sexual excitement while committing a crime is not confined to sadistic rapists. Some serial arsonists, bombers, armed robbers and burglars become sexually aroused while committing these crimes. Some of these offenders are also rapists. Arsonists who have difficulty obtaining an erection may be able to perform while watching a fire.

A serial arsonist who was sexually potent only while watching a fire, set a fire at night to an apartment complex under construction in a new subdivision. He had sex with his girlfriend in a nearby field with little risk of detection, as there was no one living in the area. Anyone who might appear would watch the fire. Another arsonist, sexually excited by the fire he set at an apartment complex under construction, told me he went to a portable toilet, provided for use by the construction workers, and masturbated. He returned more than once to the portable toilet while the fire fighters were putting out the blaze.

A young man, who set over thirty fires in a four-year period, described his sexual gratification from fire: "They've got me for arson. I have set many fires in the last several years. I just like to watch the fire. All the excitement, the smoke, the fireman working, it made me proud, very glad that I was the one who did it. It gives me a sort of sex feeling, the flame, the fire, and the color. Every time I set a fire it makes me excited" (Macdonald 1977).

The serial arsonist likes to watch his handiwork so he is likely to be in the crowd watching his fire. If he becomes sexually excited he may masturbate at the scene. Arson investigators watch and often photograph onlookers at fire scenes. The man who is masturbating is likely to be the arsonist, except in very large cities, like New York, with so many unusual people that there may be more than one person in the crowd playing with himself.

Three out of eighteen serial bombers I have interviewed told me they derived sexual gratification from their explosions. One bomber commented, "I'd rather shoot a rifle and hear the sound of explosives than ball my old lady."

Serial arsonists and serial bombers share features of the psychological profile of sadistic rapists, for example, the triad that Levin and Fox refer to as the Macdonald triad: childhood cruelty to animals, firesetting, and bed wetting.

A search warrant for the home of an armed robber and burglar revealed a large dildo underneath his mattress. The presence of this dildo suggested a need for it because of occasional impotence. His wife told me that sometimes he had difficulty obtaining an erection, but never after "pulling a job" (committing a crime). Some burglars become sexually excited when breaking and entering into a home.

William Heirens, who began stealing women's underclothing at the age of nine, was a burglar and firesetter. At the age of seventeen he assaulted a nurse and murdered two women and a six-year-old girl. "He had sexual excitement or an erection at the sight of an open window at the place to be burglarized. Going through the window he had an emission. Later it took several entrances to produce the emission. Emission was accompanied or preceded by defecation or urination. If startled in the act of burglarizing he immediately killed . . . After assaulting the nurse he had an orgasm and without striking her again he left" (Foster Kennedy et al.).

Crimes of Great Cruelty

Whenever a crime involves great cruelty one should consider the possibility of sadism. As long ago as 1911, Hans Gross, the German criminal psychologist, warned that "It will be well, in the examination of a person accused of a cruel crime, not to neglect the question of his sexual habits, or better still, to be sure to inquire particularly whether the whole situation of the crime was not sexual in nature. In a sadistic murder there may be no sexual assault and the sexual nature of the offense passes unnoticed. Yet the murderer may have obtained a sexual thrill, perhaps even orgasm, from stabbing the victim so that he is no longer interested in any possible plan for sexual assault."

The sadist may ejaculate on strangling, bludgeoning, or stabbing his victim. There need not be any sexual contact. The murderer Vincenz Verzeni experienced sexual sensations as soon as he grasped his victims by the neck. It did not matter whether the women were old, young, ugly, or beautiful. Usually simply choking them satisfied him and he then allowed his victims to live. When sexual satisfaction was delayed he continued to choke his victims until they died. Verzeni reported that his feeling of pleasure while strangling women was much greater than that which he experienced while masturbating (Krafft-Ebing).

When there is a sexual assault the sadist may find it necessary to degrade, injure, or torture his victim in order to maintain his erection. Retarded ejaculation may prevent completion of the sexual act so that no sperm are found in the victim. Sadists will torture and dissect animals as well as human beings. Cats and dogs disappear from the neighborhood.

The sadistic personality delights in cruelty, but he is not always cruel. The sadistic murderer does not kill every woman he entices into his car; the sadistic rapist does not slowly run his knife up and down the bare back of every victim; the sadistic armed robber does not pistol whip every store clerk; the sadistic burglar does not tie up and stab every home owner he encounters; and the sadistic bomber does not mail a Christmas package to all his wife's lovers. But always there is the risk of acts of great cruelty. Such cruelty may occur very rarely, or it may be a frequent feature of the M.O.

Many sadistic offenders keep committing the same type of crime over and over again. The sadistic arsonist may set fires for years and never commit any other crime. There is always the possibility that he may rape or murder. The sadistic rapist may also set a fire or blow up a building.

The criminal sadist may conceal from even the most skilful interviewers that he obtained sexual excitement from the suffering of his victims. He may talk about sexual excitement from sexual intercourse with his victims. Sexual excitement from intercourse is something most people can understand, even if they are shocked by the use of force to obtain sex. The sadist knows that if he says he is sexually excited by the pain and suffering of his victim, he is going to offend the detective and, more important, the jurors who listen to the detective's testimony.

Even after he has been convicted and sentenced he may still conceal this information because he is ashamed, because he does not want his family or some person he respects to know that he has fallen so low, or because he hopes to obtain an early release from custody by claiming a religious conversion and a successful response to treatment in prison. Even if he has been sentenced to death and all his appeals have failed, he may still hope for a last minute commutation by the governor of the state.

If a serial murderer has raped and tortured a number of women, he is probably a criminal sexual sadist regardless of whether he states that he was sexually excited by the suffering of his victims. Some rape victims report that their assailants seem to get more pleasure from seeing their great fear and terror than from the vaginal, oral, or anal sex. In these cases, the victim provides important diagnostic information that the rapist conceals.

The definition of sexual sadism may be too narrow because it demands sexual arousal from watching the suffering of the victim. In my opinion the criminal sexual sadist has a persistent pattern of gaining pleasure, even if it is not as much as he anticipated, from controlling, dominating, terrorizing, and sexually assaulting victims. He may or may not become sexually excited by the victim's suffering or by his fantasies of the victim's suffering.

This is not just an academic squabble over the wording of a definition. Failure to recognize a sadistic murderer may lead to a twenty-year sentence, and a sadistic murderer is back on the streets looking for more women to kill within ten years. The first murder may not appear to involve torture, and there may be no evidence from the crime scene to point to sadism, but review of past convictions or a thorough background evaluation of the man may point to his sadistic personality and great dangerousness.

The diagnosis of sadism should not be applied automatically to anyone who commits an unusually cruel assault or murder, as for example:

Group rapists who inflict terrible injuries on their victim. Individual members, with a need to prove themselves, add to the victim's injuries with horrifying fatal results.

Murderers intent on revenge who cruelly murder a wife, the wife's children or her lover.

Murderers who dismember the body after death. Cutting up the body may be part of an attempt to transport the body to avoid detection. Far from gaining pleasure, the offender may find the task most distasteful. A female murderer told me that only after nightfall with the lights off, could she cut up her victim, because she had difficulty looking at his body. This man had attempted to rape her.

Organized crime hit men. These men are required to kill as a condition of their employment.

Psychotic offenders acting under the influence of delusional beliefs, who commit cruel murders, for example, through crucifixion.

Nazi concentration camp guards who tortured and killed Jews with the encouragement of their superior officers.

Police officers in repressive regimes who torture prisoners, sometimes with fatal consequences, to obtain confessions to crimes, especially crimes against the government.

Soldiers in war time who commit atrocities against prisoners of war or civilians of the country at war. After World War II, a Japanese soldier, when questioned about cruelty to British prisoners of war, told me, "To be cruel is to be loyal to the emperor."

Terrorists and Freedom Fighters. The label depends on whose side you support. Persons who belong to these groups will kill when ordered to do so out of loyalty to their cause. Many revolutionary groups strongly disapprove of rape by their members, or by anyone else. In Northern Ireland during "The Troubles" with the Irish Republican Army, members of outlawed groups, both protestant and catholic, knee capped (a bullet fired from behind through the knee) civilian rapists.

Some of the groups described above may include sadists, who join the group because of the opportunities to commit sadistic acts.

CHILDHOOD ABUSE OF SERIAL RAPISTS

There is a frequent history of childhood physical, sexual, and verbal abuse in the background of serial rapists. Often this information is surprisingly difficult to obtain, especially when one considers how often today children are accusing or falsely accusing their parents of physical, sexual, and Satanic abuse. The abuse excuse is becoming popular in the courtroom and in sex offender treatment programs. Other males and females with access to children may also abuse them. The person who abuses the child may not be an adult, but an older sibling or fellow school student.

Physical Abuse

Physical abuse, especially by a parent, provides a role model for the child and also generates aggression. I have encountered rapists who were given repeated enemas at intervals over many months.

Sexual Abuse

Both fathers and mothers may sexually abuse their sons. Other persons, as described above, may also sexually assault children, both in and outside the home. Some fathers abuse only their daughters, but such abuse can have a very adverse effect on the sons as well as on the daughters. Both fathers and mothers can contribute to a son's abnormal sexual development by failing to show disapproval of any abnormal sexual behavior. Mothers can abuse a child through seductive behavior toward the child, and open promiscuity.

Seductive Behavior

The seductive mother arouses overwhelming anxiety in her son and great anger which may be expressed directly toward her but more often is displaced on to other women. Maternal seductive behavior includes dressing and undressing in front of a son, walking around nude or in underclothing, especially see-through blouses or nighties. The mother may leave the bathroom door open while in the bath, then ask her son to bring her soap or a towel, perhaps even talking to him at length. Most sons are aware that this is not commonly accepted behavior, and the effect on them is different than in those tropical cultures where women do not cover their breasts.

The mother who showers with her son invites trouble. The mother who encourages her son, regardless of his age, to sleep with her whenever her husband is away from home is not doing him a favor. If her husband dies, the oldest male child may be asked to take over father's role; this should not include sleeping with mother.

Easson and Steinhilber reported that among seven children and adolescents who showed murderous aggression, lack of privacy, physical overcloseness and, at times, the grossest seductions were repeatedly found. For example, the mother of one thirteen-year-old boy had for five or six years been in the habit of getting into bed with the boy and, face to face with him, massaging his back.

The mother of another thirteen-year-old boy gave him details of her first intercourse. Repeatedly this boy had pleaded for firm discipline and definite limit setting. Despite his murderous outbursts and his requests for control, he was allowed to retain his collection of knives and guns.

Repeatedly the parents indicated to this boy that they expected from him aggressive and dangerous behavior.

From age twelve, he had asked his mother repeated questions about her sexual activities. On many occasions he asked if he could have intercourse with her. Her standard answer was, "Yes, but it would be horrible." The boy obtained from his mother details of her first intercourse and details as to how she felt during intercourse when his sister was conceived. The father thought that perhaps the boy might rape his mother.

Father, not mother, should provide sex instruction for the male children. Certainly mother should not comment on her husband's sexual performance, talk about her periods, and show her son how to use a condom. If incest occurs, it may be very difficult to obtain this information from either mother or son.

Promiscuous Behavior

The parent who is openly promiscuous may create great problems for the children. The son who sees or hears what goes on when mother brings men home, may become sexually aroused and then frustrated. There is often very great anger at mother because she is disloyal to father, and if father is dead or divorced there is anger arising from his own sexual arousal and guilt over such feelings.

Failure to Discourage Inappropriate Behavior

Parents who overlook inappropriate sexual behavior encourage such behavior. Some parents seem not to be aware of their failure to set limits, or they may set limits then fail to enforce them. The child may be given mixed messages. Johnson and Robinson give examples of vacillation, ambiguity, equivocation, or double-talk on the part of parents. "A request to 'sonny' to wear his bathrobe becomes ineffective when coupled with mother's 'cute' reference to the charms of the boy's nudity ... A transvestite boy of fourteen years of age, at the age of five, had been found smelling assorted laundry items belonging to his mother. Instead of an unequivocal prohibition, the mother urged only that the boy substitute her clean underclothing."

"Children sense the anxious, vacillating permission and seduction in such parental double-talk. Another manifestation of double-talk is the

parentally-expressed concern for imagined future misdeeds by the child—
the imagination deriving from the parent's mind but taking root in that
of the child. There may be dire warnings of future sexual misconduct
quite foreign to the child's conscious inclinations. A consciously guileless
adolescent who is subjected to suspicious, suggestive, unfriendly quiz-
zing angrily apprehends the destructive lack of faith on the part of the
parent. The child senses that he is expected to misbehave sexually. The
parent's fantasy that their small child will probably get into sexual
trouble during adolescence provides a compelling guide. Unconsciously,
the parents gradually maneuver this child into adolescent sexual acting
out."

Verbal Abuse

Calling a son a faggot, a queer, a pansy, a pimp, a pinhead, a shithead,
and an asshole is not likely to improve his self-esteem nor are some of the
words likely to aid in his sexual adjustment. This son killed his father.

The Domineering Mother

Some serial rapists come from a home dominated by a very controlling
mother with a weak or absent father, or from a home with a mother,
several sisters, and no brothers. In the family home the serial rapist is a
milquetoast; in his victim's home he is in total control. His victim may
resemble his mother in appearance, bossiness, or other mannerisms, but
not usually in age.

The Inadequate or Absent Father

Lisak and Roth suggest a greater role for the father in the etiology of
rape-associated dynamics than has previously been reported. Statements
about their parents, by a group of self-reported rapists, suggested almost
uniformly negative relationships with their fathers. Father's abdication
of his role in the family left the son trapped in an intensified relationship
with his mother, without the support he needs from his father to
maneuver his way out of the nest and into a secure masculine identification.

RESEARCH ON PHYSICAL AND
SEXUAL ABUSE OF CHILDREN

Many reports on murderers and violent rape offenders tend to support the viewpoint that violence begets violence. Many clinicians who interview violent criminals are impressed by the frequency of physical and sexual abuse in their childhood. Widom, who has reviewed research on the cycle of violence, concludes that being abused or neglected as a child increases one's risk for delinquency, adult criminal behavior, and violent criminal behavior. However, the majority of abused and neglected children do not become delinquent, criminal, or violent.

Widom points out the shortcomings of much of the research: small sample sizes, weak sampling techniques, questionable accuracy of information, and lack of appropriate comparison groups. She notes the need for research on possible protective factors that may buffer some children from the long-term negative effects of childhood abuse.

Heredity and Environment

Both genetic and environmental factors contribute to antisocial behavior. The father with an antisocial personality might well abuse and neglect his children. Such abuse and neglect could add to any genetic influence on the children's personality development. Crowley and Riggs draw attention to research on this issue.

For example, Frick et al. (1992) found that, in comparison with controls, boys with conduct disorder were significantly more likely to have mothers who provided poor supervision and inconsistent discipline. In addition, these boys were significantly more likely to have fathers with antisocial personality disorder, and when that paternal influence was controlled statistically, the maternal behaviors contributed little to the risk of developing conduct disorder.

Crowe (1972) found that twenty-five-year-old, adopted-out offspring of mothers in prison were more likely to have arrest records, convictions, and incarcerations than adopted-out controls whose mothers had not been in prison. Such data strongly support the view that the offspring's criminality was biologically influenced by the mothers' criminality, since the mothers had little psychological influence on their adopted-out children.

Grove et al. (1990) examined identical twins who were reared apart from early in life, counting the number of antisocial symptoms which these people reported both in childhood and in adulthood. There were significant correlations within twin pairs; if one twin had numerous antisocial behaviors, the other was likely to follow suit. Since the twins were raised apart such correlations probably could not arise from a shared environment. This study and others cited by Crowley and Riggs strongly suggest that delinquent and criminal behavior are under some genetic control.

Farrington (1991), in a prospective longitudinal survey of over 400 inner-city London boys, found that high levels of aggression at age eight predicted later violent delinquency. Violent delinquents were significantly more likely to have cruel, criminal parents. Monahan, drawing on research by Farrington and others, states that while many aggressive children go on to be law-abiding adults, aggression at age eight significantly predicts violent convictions well into the thirties, in every culture in which it has been studied.

MOTIVATIONS OF THE RAPE OFFENDER

Although sex would seem to be an obvious and important motive in rape, many authorities consider that power and anger overshadow sexuality. Groth, for example, states: "Rape is first and foremost an aggressive offense, prompted more by anger and power than by desire. It is a pseudosexual act. It is sexual behavior in the service of nonsexual needs" (Groth p. 1358).

Rapists are classified by Groth et al. as:

"The *power assertive rapist* regards rape as an expression of his virility and mastery and dominance. He feels entitled to 'take it' or sees sexual domination as a way of keeping 'his' women in line. The rape is a reflection of the inadequacy he experiences in terms of his sense of identity and effectiveness.

"The *power reassurance rapist* commits the offense in an effort to resolve disturbing doubts about his sexual adequacy and masculinity. He wants to place a woman in a helpless, controlled position in which she cannot refuse or reject him, thereby shoring up his failing sense of worth and adequacy.

"The *anger-retaliation rapist* commits rape as an expression of his hostility and rage towards women. His motive is revenge and his aim is degradation and humiliation.

"The **anger-excitation rapist** finds pleasure, thrills, and excitation in the suffering of his victim. He is sadistic and his aim is to punish, hurt, and torture his victim" (Groth et al.).

These authors state that "Rape is more than an illegal act and more than an extreme of cultural role behavior. From a clinical point of view, it is important that rape be defined as a sexual deviation and that the pathology of the offender be recognized" (Groth et al.). Profiles of rapists are described in Chapter 8.

FEMINIST VIEWPOINT: RAPE IS NOT A SEX CRIME

Susan Brownmiller, a noted feminist, makes her view clear: "From prehistoric times to the present, I believe, rape has played a critical function. It is nothing more or less than a conscious process of intimidation by which all men keep all women in a state of fear." This does seem to be an overstatement; yet many feminists share Brownmiller's viewpoint that women are victims of male power. The rapist on the street, the office manager who sexually harasses his secretary, and the violent husband in the home all exert this power.

The emphasis on the weakness of women and the power of men has merit, but many women in everyday conversation make it clear that they are in charge and no one can trifle with them. Whether they are talking to a clerk in a store or to a business associate, they speak with authority and will neither tolerate delay nor specious excuses for failure to meet their demands.

Many women hold senior executive posts in both private business and in government offices and there have been reports of female office managers abusing their power over male subordinates. In California a company was ordered to pay $1,000,000 compensation and damages to its former financial manager, Sabino Guiterrez, for sexual harassment over a period of six years by Mary Martinez, the company's chief financial officer. She had requested "kisses and coupling" without his enthusiastic consent.

The court was told that Mary Martinez was peeved when Guiterrez got married and she trashed his office while he was on honeymoon. Lyndon, who sees this court judgment as the beginning of the end for modern feminism, commented: "Such is the terrifying wrath of a woman spurned; rejected mistresses slash your clothes, slighted bosses wreck your work space . . . the truth is that women who are appointed to positions of power at work are just as likely as men to take advantage of their power to advance a sexual interest in their subordinates. Women are just as likely as men to fiddle their expense accounts for someone they fancy, to fix a promotion or to turn a benevolent or forgiving eye on absenteeism or lousy time-keeping."

There are many women who believe that rape is a sex crime. Camille Paglia takes a strong stand on this issue. "For a decade, feminists have drilled their disciples to say 'Rape is a crime of violence but not of sex.' This sugar-coated Shirley Temple nonsense has exposed young women to disaster. Misled by feminism, they do not expect rape from the nice boys from good homes who sit next to them in class."

Lee Ellis points out that at least among date rapists, many of the actions taken toward victims are highly suggestive of sexual motivation. These actions include attempting to get their dates drunk, lying about loving them and using other forms of deceit, arguing and pressuring dates to "give in," threatening to break off relationships and ignoring protests as they attempt to undress the victims. Physical force is often used only after nonviolent tactics have failed.

Most date rapists are motivated by a desire for sex rather than wanting to show their power over their victims or over women in general. Both men and women assign less blame to a rapist if the victim was dressed in sexually provocative clothing. Ellis comments that it would be difficult to account for this without assuming that sexuality is important to rape motivation.

HOMOSEXUALITY AND RAPE

It has been suggested that latent or overt homosexuality contributes to rape. According to this theory, the man has to prove to himself that he is not a homosexual by repeated acts of intercourse with willing or unwilling women. Halleck notes that quite frequently in our society latent homosexual fears are associated with paranoid attitudes toward the world and particularly toward females, who threaten the homosexual's masculine image. The rapist tends to see all women as seductive, depriving, and dangerous. He frequently vacillates between perceiving them as frightening giantesses or as lesser beings. In his attacks upon women, he both conquers his fears and confirms their inferiority.

Many rapists do give a history of homosexual behavior or thoughts and temptations. Alternatively their aversion to any physical contact, however slight, with other men; excessive anger at homosexuals or their great delight in encouraging homosexuals to make advances then beating them savagely, suggest an over reaction based upon their conscious or unconscious fear of this tendency within themselves.

One rapist, unsure of his masculinity, joined the Marine Corps, to prove "I was a man." He worried that his penis was small (not true) and in his rapes he feared that he would be unable to satisfy his victims. Twice a year he arranged for a sperm count and despite reassuring reports he ruminated over his failure to impregnate his girlfriend over a period of two years. She became pregnant shortly after her marriage to another man. When another girlfriend refused to marry him because she wanted to go to college, he felt that the real reason for her refusal was because "she thought my intercourse was no good. She wanted something better."

He described his mother as a "sexy babe with a big bosom," his wife as "she's just like my mother, like two peas in a pod, always telling me what's best for me, her waist is real small like my mother's," and his victims as "sexy looking, filled out real nice." He said that his mother dyed her hair blond when he started dating blond girls. She objected to his choice of girlfriends, saying they were just tramps, and she showed great interest in his activities outside the home and was always wondering if he was on a date. He had fantasies of cutting off the breasts of his victims, and he mentioned that he would enjoy having a room in which breasts were mounted like trophies on the wall. "I don't know how you could mount a vagina. How could you cut a vagina off?"

THE MEN WHO RAPE

Offenders include men with or without sexual deviations and personality disorders. Some have an antisocial personality or sadistic personality. The inadequate as well as the borderline or schizoid personality may take by force that which he cannot obtain through his poor social graces and his lack of confidence in himself. The man with an alleged multiple personality disorder, presently a fashionable diagnosis in some clinics, may blame one of his many personalities. An offender may have more than one diagnosis; for example, the antisocial personality may also have a sadistic personality along with sexual deviations.

Many men accused of rape may have no psychiatric disorder. Only a small percentage of sex offenders have a psychosis such as paranoid schizophrenia. A few rapists have presenile brain disorders and some are mentally retarded.

THE ANTISOCIAL PERSONALITY

The antisocial personality, sometimes called a psychopathic or sociopathic personality, may seize an opportunity to commit any offense. He will take your money, your car, or your wife. If his needs of the moment include rape, he may not care whether his victim is a child, a cripple, or an elderly woman. Almost four out of five prisoners in penitentiaries are antisocial personalities. This is not surprising as the diagnosis is based largely on a history of antisocial and criminal behavior.

There are antisocial personalities who have never been arrested and who conceal their criminal and other antisocial activities from interviewers, even from skilled interviewers. Their parents and friends may know, yet they too may conceal this information from outsiders. Even if one of them talks, no one may listen, so convincing is the clever psychopath, who may be a police officer, lawyer, doctor, teacher, senior army officer, politician or successful business man. The fact that someone is regarded as an outstanding citizen does not rule out the possibility that he is a psychopath or a rape suspect. The talented psychopath is either on the board of directors or in the joint.

He is the serial killer and youth molester John Gacy who was photographed standing alongside Rosalyn Carter, when her husband was President. He is serial killer and rapist Ted Bundy, the law student who was a volunteer working for the re-election of the Republican governor of the state of Washington.

Psychopaths are impulsive, irresponsible, self-centered people who live as if there is no tomorrow. They care not for the social and legal restrictions of everyday life and resent those in authority, yet they like to boss other people.

They seem not to have a conscience and may commit the most brutal crimes without showing any feelings of guilt or remorse. Indeed, in the courtroom, a psychopath may laugh and joke about the callous, unprovoked slaying of an elderly couple during a burglary in their home. A young armed robber, when informed of his father's death responded, "What else is new?" A few weeks later he shocked the penitentiary chaplain by reacting to news of his mother's death with the nonchalant inquiry, "Where's the insurance money?"

Psychopaths have difficulty holding a job unless it offers constant change and action with little direct supervision. The army overseas in wartime, long distance truck driving (his wife has to take care of the children and he is relieved of many responsibilities that face fathers who live at home), and flying planes to smuggle drugs from South America are among occupations that appeal to the psychopath. Some psychopaths do have good work records.

Although outwardly very independent, rebellious people, they are in fact very dependent on others. You can take advantage of their need for attention and respect in talking to them. They make friends easily, but have difficulty maintaining friendships because they demand much and give little in return. A long-suffering wife may continue to support her psychopathic husband financially over many years of a stormy troubled marriage.

Like a child called to account for some misdeed, the psychopath points the finger of blame elsewhere. Any failure in life, loss of a job, financial reverse, divorce, or arrest for a criminal act is attributed to an unjust employer, a heartless wife, incompetent teachers, unloving parents, or society in general. Curiously, even if the psychopath may have good reason to blame his parents for childhood neglect or physical abuse, he may persist in speaking of them almost exclusively in loving and grateful terms. This may occur even if he has murdered one of them.

Those psychopaths with an impressive appearance, a gift of the gab, and an ability to inspire confidence make good used car dealers and con artists. On the other hand, some psychopaths look disreputable and, far from inspiring confidence, create an immediate feeling of distrust. Even if his appearance is scruffy, he may still be able to fool others. A widely respected sheriff complained that he had been unable to cash a check in a store despite satisfactory identification, yet a psychopathic bad-check passer managed to do so despite his shabby clothing, inadequate identification and an out-of-state check.

The term manipulation is used to refer to the psychopath's skill in persuading others to do what he wants, whether through charm, flattery, fast talk, promises, deceit, threats or arousal of feelings of guilt ("If you don't help me, I'll lose my job").

They tell the most outrageous lies without blinking, even when these lies serve no useful purpose. Cleckley gives this example in *The Mask Of*

Sanity: A psychopathic husband, already divorced by his wife, wrote in a letter to her, matter-of-fact instructions about the insurance policies he was sending separately to provide for her and their children. There were no insurance policies and he had never seriously considered providing for his family in this way or any other. He was well aware that his lie would soon be found out, and he had nothing to gain materially by doing such a thing.

Disregard for the truth is not seen in their every statement. Despite their lack of conscience, not all their checks bounce, not all their promises remain unfulfilled, and at times they can show concern for the welfare of others. Some psychopaths are delightful rogues, full of good stories, and entertaining drinking companions, but don't invite them to your home, don't lend them any money.

When interviewing the psychopath, keep in mind that he will conceal information or provide false answers. For example, he may say that he has held three jobs since leaving school. If you start with his first job listing his age and date of employment, and then move on to other jobs with age and date, you may find that he remembers 30 jobs. He tells you that he served two years in the Navy and reached the rank of petty officer but his Navy records show that he was discharged within a year. All too often the claims of a psychopath are accepted at face value (Macdonald and Michaud).

ALCOHOL AND RAPE

> *Drink, sir, is a good provoker . . . Lechery, sir, it provokes and unprovokes: it provokes the desire, but it takes away the performance.*
>
> Shakespeare, *Macbeth*

> *Drunkenness does not create vice; it merely brings it into view.*
>
> Seneca

The role of alcohol in rape is difficult to evaluate. It would be helpful to have the results of breath or blood alcohol tests on one-hundred consecutive rapists. As over 45 percent of forcible rapes in the United States are not cleared by arrest, it is clearly impossible to check, with any degree of confidence, the relationship between rape and alcohol. Shupe found that of forty-two persons arrested during or immediately after the commission of rape in Columbus, Ohio, twenty-one had alcohol in their urine. This finding should be interpreted with caution, as offenders under the influence of alcohol may be less skillful in avoiding detection than sober colleagues in crime.

Rada consistently has found that 50 percent of rapists were drinking at the time of the commission of the offense, the great majority of whom were drinking heavily, defined as ten or more beers or the equivalent. In addition, 33 percent were alcoholic by history, using stringent criteria.

Alcohol impairs judgment and diminishes self-control. Yet many men drink, but relatively few of them rape. Many criminal offenses are assumed to be due to alcohol on insufficient grounds. Excessive use of alcohol and criminal behavior may have the same root cause in psychological conflict. It would be illogical to assume that because a person was drinking, prior to the offense, the act was the product of alcohol. Some offenders who rape when they are drunk also rape when they are sober.

DRUGS AND RAPE

Some drugs reduce the sexual drive; for example, the heroin addict on the nod has no interest in sex. Other drugs are reputed to increase the sexual drive, but their effectiveness seldom matches their reputation. The power of suggestion may be an important factor so that the expectation of sexual prowess results in greater sexual activity.

Stimulant drugs such as amphetamines and cocaine increase the sex drive in some people but may delay ejaculation or orgasm. Small doses of the less powerful tranquilizers, barbiturates, and marijuana may, like alcohol, reduce inhibitions or lead to a heightened interest in sex. In larger doses or with continued heavy use of some of these drugs there may be a reduction of sexual drive or even impotence. Cocaine abusers who report more enjoyable sex eventually lose all interest in sex while addicted to this drug. A number of victims have reported rape at crack houses. Often the man will claim that the victim promised sex in return for cocaine.

Hallucinogens such as LSD and PCP or angel dust do not seem to affect the sex drive, although mixed effects have been reported. In Sidney Cohen's studies of more than a thousand subjects who used the hallucinogen LSD, no sexual acting-out occurred and many reported that the LSD experience made sex irrelevant. I examined one man who attempted to rape a woman while under the influence of LSD, and later attempted rape after taking PCP. However, he also attempted to rape yet another woman when he was not under the influence of drugs.

PORNOGRAPHY AND MEDIA VIOLENCE

We cannot remain consistent and claim that pornographic images exert no influence while claiming that advertising images do.

S.J. Eysenck and D.K.B. Nias.
Sex, Violence and the Media.

The United States Commission on Obscenity and Pornography (1970) found no evidence to show that pornography is harmful. The Attorney General's Commission on Pornography (1986) disagreed. It is not easy to determine scientifically the effects of pornography and media violence on behavior and much quoted research studies have been criticized for one or more shortcomings. Repeated exposure to sex and violence on television and in movies can hardly have an ennobling effect on viewers. We become desensitized to sex and violence.

"Audiences once titillated by the sight of a bare thigh on a can-can dancer are now bored by sexual gymnastics performed by today's motion picture actors. So it is with violence, and like pornography, its level of intensity must constantly be increased to sustain our interest. Networks warn us that their programs may contain violent scenes unsuitable for children. But like the R ratings in movies, they only attract more viewers" (Amole).

Studies have shown that rape rates increased dramatically in some countries after enactment of more liberal laws on pornography. Two states in Australia had similar rape rates until liberalization of pornography laws in one state resulted in an increase in the rape rate in that state. Return to more conservative laws in Hawaii and New Zealand was followed by a reduction in the rape rates.

In the United States, Baron and Straus found that the higher the circulation rate of sex magazines in a state, the higher the rape rate. These authors are extremely hesitant to interpret their findings as reflecting a cause-effect relationship between pornography and rape. They think that both higher rape rates and the higher circulation of sex magazines are due to a macho culture pattern that favors the use of physical force to settle quarrels, a belief in male superiority and approval of sexual coercion. A greater magnitude of this cultural orientation in some states than in others could influence men both to purchase more pornography and to commit rape.

Pornography does not cause sexual deviation but does play a role in the lives of sexual deviates and may provoke an act of rape. Murrin and Laws in a review of research on pornography conclude that non sex offenders tend to outgrow pornography in adolescence, whereas pornography becomes increasingly important to many sex offenders after they become adults. Pornography plays a much more important role in the life of the pedophile than in the life of the rapist. Pornography arouses both offenders and nonoffenders, but rapists are also aroused by pornography that includes the use of force. If the victim appears to be "enjoying" the rape, male college students may also be aroused.

Detective magazines have been described as pornography for the sexual sadist. The cover photographs often show men standing over women secured with ropes, chains or handcuffs. Guns, knives, blood, and frightened, partially undressed women with accentuated breasts combine sex and violence. Park Dietz et al. reported that nineteen detective magazines provided information on techniques for committing crimes and published advertisements for weapons, burglary tools, car theft equipment, police badges, and false identification.

To top off their helpful hints for rapists and murderers the magazines described the errors of offenders leading to their arrest and the investigative methods of detectives. The authors state that sexual sadists are particularly drawn to these magazines and some of them translate their fantasies into action. One multiple murderer had a collection of detective magazine covers.

REFERENCES

American Psychiatric Association: *Diagnostic and Statistical Manual of Mental Disorders,* Fourth Edition. Washington, DC, American Psychiatric Association, 1994.

Amole, Gene: Preaching Jesus, allowing violence. *Rocky Mountain News,* October 14, 1993.

Attorney General's Commission on Pornography: *Final Report.* Washington, DC, US Department of Justice, 1986.

Baron, Larry and Straus, M.A.: *Four Theories of Rape in American Society.* New Haven, Yale University Press, 1989.

Brownmiller S *Against Our Will.* New York, Simon and Schuster, 1975.

Cleckley, Hervey: *The Mask of Sanity.* St. Louis, Mosby, 1964.

Cohen, Sydney. *The Substance Abuse Problems.* New York, Haworth Press, 1981.

Crowe, R.R.: The adopted offspring of women criminal offenders. *Arch Gen Psychiat, 28:*600, 1972.

Crowley, T.J., and Riggs, P.D.: Adolescent substance use disorder with conduct disorder, and comorbid conditions. In Rahdert, E (Ed.): *Adolescent Drug Abuse: Clinical Assessment and Therapeutic Intervention.* NIDA Monograph Series, In Press.

Dietz, P.E., Harry, B., Hazelwood, R.R.: Detective magazines: Pornography for the sexual sadist? *J. For Sci, 31:*197, 1986.

Easson, W.M., and Steinhilber, R.M.: Murderous aggression by children and adolescents. *Arch Gen Psychiat, 4:*27, 1961.

Ellis, Lee: A synthesized (biosocial) theory of rape. *J. Consult Clin Psychol, 59:*631, 1991.

Eysenck, H.J., and Nias, D.K.B.: *Sex, Violence and the Media.* London, Temple Smith, 1978.

Farrington, D.P.: The family background of aggressive youths. In Hersov, L.A. *et al Aggression and Antisocial Behavior in Childhood and Adolescence.* New York, Pergamon Press, 1978.

Ferenczi, S.: *Further Contributions to the Theory and Technique of Psychoanalysis.* London, Hogarth, 1926.

Frick, P.J., Lahey, B.B., *et al:* Familial risk factors to oppositional defiant disorder and conduct disorder. *J Consult Clin Psychol, 60:*49, 1992.

Gross, Hans: *Criminal Psychology.* Boston, Little Brown, 1915.

Groth, A.N.: *Men Who Rape.* New York, Plenum, 1979.

Groth, A.N.: Book Review, *Am. J. Psychiat, 136;* 1358, 1979.

Groth, A.N., Burgess, A.W., and Holmstrom, L.L.: Rape, power, anger and sexuality. *Amer. J. Psychiat, 134:*1329, 1977.

Grove, W.W., Eckert, E.D., *et al.:* Heritability of substance abuse and antisocial behavior. *Biol Psychiat, 27:*1293, 1990.

Halleck, S.L.: *Psychiatry and the Dilemmas of Crime.* New York, Harper, 1967.

Hazelwood, R.R., Dietz, P.E. and Warren, Janet, The Criminal Sexual Sadist. *FBI Law Enforcement Bull.* February, 1992.

Johnson, A.M., and Robinson, D.B.: The sexual deviant (sexual psychopath)—causes, treatment and prevention. *JAMA, 164:*1559, 1957.

Kennedy, Foster et al. A study of William Heirens. *Amer J Psychiat, 104,* 113, 1947.

Krafft-Ebing, Richard. *Psychopathia Sexualis.* Chicago, W.T. Keener, 1900.

Levin, Jack and Fox, J.A.: *Mass Murder.* New York, Plenum Press, 1985.

Lisak, David and Roth, Susan: Motives and psychodynamics of self-reported, unincarcerated rapists. *Amer J Orthopsychiat, 60:*268, 1990.

Lyndon, Neil. Come up and sue me sometime. *Sunday Times,* (London), May 30, 1993.

Macdonald, J.M.: *Bombers and Firesetters.* Springfield, C.C. Thomas, 1977.

Macdonald, J.M.: *The Murderer and His Victim.* 2nd ed. Springfield, C.C. Thomas, 1986.

Monahan, John,: The causes of violence. *FBI Law Enforcement Bull,* January, 1994.

Murrin M.R., and Laws D.R.: The influence of pornography on sexual crimes. In

Marshall, W.L., Laws, D.R., and Barbaree, H.E.: *Handbook of Sexual Assault: Issues theories and treatment of the offender.* New York, Plenum Press, 1990.

Paglia, C.: *Sex, Art & American Culture.* Vintage 1992.

Rada, R.T.: *Clinical Aspects of the Rapist.* New York, Grune and Stratton, 1978.

Shupe, L.M.: Alcohol and crime. *J Crim Law, 44:*661, 1954.

West, D.J.: *Sexual Crimes & Confrontations.* Aldershot, Gower 1987.

Widom, C.P.: The cycle of violence. *Science, 244:* 160, 1989.

Chapter 3

DATE, ACQUAINTANCE, AND GROUP RAPE

DATE RAPE

Take Consent Forms and a Breathalyser

As far as I am concerned, you can change your mind before, even during, but not just after sex.

Martin Amis

Date rape can be as brutal and violent as rape by a stranger. Date rape can also be something less than rape. A woman wakes up with a hangover in a young man's bed and says to herself, "Oh no!" Is the man who persuaded her to have sex a rapist? A young man wakes up with a hangover, sees the frumpy, middle-aged woman beside him, and says to himself "Never again!" Is the woman who talked him into sex a rapist?

Both a man and his girlfriend use poor judgment after a few glasses of alcohol. If both are under the weather, should we blame the man and excuse the woman? Where is the equality of the sexes? It might be different if one drinks a weak mix and serves the other only strong mixed drinks. One is sober and calculating, the other is naive and under the table.

Date rapes are especially likely to go unreported. Victims blame themselves for misjudging the character of a boyfriend, are too embarrassed, or feel that nothing will be accomplished in the courtroom. They know that they will be put on trial. They are discouraged by the results of much publicized date rape trials. In the absence of bodily injury or the evidence of a witness, everything hinges on consent. The issue becomes who is telling the truth: the accused or the accuser. In stranger-rape, when the rapist breaks into a home, it is obvious that there is no consent.

It has been suggested that there should be special date rape laws, but critics say that such laws would practically require a man to obtain a signed affidavit from a woman before having sex with her. A Canadian business sells sexual consent forms to men who fear being falsely accused of rape or sexual harassment. Besides attesting that both parties are agreeable, cosigners can list where sex occurred, the birth control method, and if either partner was using drugs or alcohol. Newspaper advertisements for sexual consent forms warn "Dating can be dangerous. Protect yourself."

DATE AND ACQUAINTANCE RAPE

Mary Koss Ph.D. and her team of associates administered a self-report questionnaire to 3,187 female college students enrolled in technical schools, community colleges, Ivy League schools, and state universities (Koss et al. 1987). They found that 27.5 percent, one in four of these college students, had been the victims of rape or attempted rape since the age of fourteen. Koss headed the Ms national research project on date and acquaintance rape, and Robin Warshaw has provided additional statistics on the survey of the 3,187 female college students.

Although most victims never reported the attacks, 84 percent knew the men who raped them and 57 percent of the rapes happened on dates. Thus most of the rapes were acquaintance or date rapes. *Indeed, 42 percent of the women who were raped said they had sex again with the men who assaulted them* (Warshaw).

One-quarter of the women thought it was rape; one-quarter thought it was some kind of crime but did not realize it qualified as rape; one-quarter thought it was serious sexual abuse but did not know it qualified as a crime; and one-quarter did not feel victimized by the experience (Koss, 1992).

About 8 percent of the 2,971 college men in the survey reported that they had raped or attempted to rape a woman sometime since the age of fourteen. Fifty-five percent of the men who raped said they had sex again with the victims (Warshaw). Thus 42 percent of the victims and 55 percent of the offenders entered into consenting sexual relationships after the rape!

There have been criticisms of this study. Neil Gilbert, professor of social welfare at the University of California at Berkeley comments: "If we accept the number of students raped in just one year, according to Ms. survey researcher Mary Koss's definition, then over a four-year period, about 25 percent of female students will be raped, and half of these women will be victimized twice. An additional 40 percent of female students will be victims of attempted rape, and more than half of this group will be victimized twice. All together, over four years almost two-thirds of female college students will suffer an incident of rape or attempted rape, and most of these victims will be victimized more than once."

Gilbert notes that the figures are seldom reported this way because advocates recognize that there is a limit to which Congress and the public will suspend belief even in the face of purportedly expert opinion.

Koss has responded to criticism by pointing out that rape prevalence estimates in the range of 15–25 percent have been reported in seven large scale studies including women in Minnesota, San Francisco, Los Angeles, Cleveland, and Charleston (Koss, 1992). We cannot, however, assume that a woman was raped because she makes that claim in a telephone interview with a research worker or in a written response to a questionnaire.

Feminists have confidence in these surveys, but Barbara Amiel suspects bias in their viewpoint: "Ideally, feminists would prefer to spare women the bother of testifying in rape cases at all, and would simply send the accused a notice informing him of the charge of rape and requiring him to turn up for sentencing."

Rape rates based on the statements of alleged victims without investigation of the allegations, have obvious shortcomings. Nevertheless, date and acquaintance rape often do not come to the attention of the police and much of the research on rape offenders has been based largely upon studies of men who have raped strangers.

Kanin studied 71 white, undergraduate students who admitted date-rape. Only six were certain that they had been reported to the police, and in every case the victim refused to prosecute. Seven cases were not included because the relationships with the victims persisted for at least four months after the "rape." In all these cases, consensual intercourse became routine. Kanin suggested that in these instances the female could only placate her guilt at entering into coitus by claiming the use of force and duress. The violence did not involve threats with weapons. Fists were used in only four cases. There was heavy reliance on the physical overpowering of the female, which Kanin described as mismatched wrestling contests.

WOMEN WHO SAY NO WHEN THEY MEAN YES

Muehlenhard and Hollabaugh investigated whether 610 undergraduate women ever engaged in token resistance to sex, saying no but meaning yes. The women were asked in a questionnaire if and how often they had indicated to a man that they did not want to have sex even though they had every intention to and were willing to engage in sexual intercourse.

They found that 39.3 percent reported saying no when they meant yes. Of these women, 32.5 percent did it once, 45.6 percent did it two to five times, 11.2 percent did it six to ten times, 7.8 percent reported eleven to twenty times, and 2.9 percent reported more than twenty times.

Of those women who had said no when they meant yes, 85.2 percent had done so within the past year. Among sexually experienced women, 60.8 percent had said no when they meant yes, compared with 11.9 percent of sexually inexperienced women. Although the latter group of women had been willing and intended to engage in sexual intercourse, the men involved apparently believed their refusals and stopped making sexual advances.

The reasons for saying no when they meant yes included:

Practical reasons:
I didn't want him to think I was easy or loose.
I didn't want to appear too aggressive or eager.
I was afraid of his telling other people.
I was afraid I might get a venereal disease.
I was afraid I might get pregnant.
There were other people around.

Emotional, religious, or moral concerns:
I wasn't ready for it emotionally.
It was against my religious beliefs.
It was against my moral values.

Fear of physical discomfort:
I was afraid it would hurt.
I wasn't sure how it would feel or that I'd like how it felt.

Manipulative:
I wanted him to be more physically aggressive.
I wanted him to talk me into it.
I wanted him to beg.

I wanted to get him more sexually aroused by making him wait.
I was angry with him and wanted to get back at him.
I wanted to be in control—to be the one to decide when.

Muehlenhard and Hollabaugh emphasize that: "First, most women (60.7 percent) reported that they had never engaged in token resistance, and over three-fourths of the women who had engaged in token resistance reported doing so five or fewer times. Thus, when a woman says no, chances are that she means it. Second, regardless of the incidence of token resistance, if the woman means no and the man persists, it is rape."

MARITAL RAPE

Most state laws now provide for conviction and punishment of a man for raping his wife. Women Against Rape, writing collectively in the *New Law Journal* in 1990, claimed that rape by husbands is just as painful and traumatic as rape by strangers, in some ways worse. Carol Sarler comments that these ladies overlook factors that generally are absent from an attack by a husband. These factors include fear of what would be an intolerable pregnancy, fear of AIDS, and the blinding terror that every breath breathed is the last . . . a terror whose enduring trauma can blight an entire life.

GROUP RAPE

Birds of a feather flock together.

Group rape can be an especially terrifying and humiliating experience. The girl who is seized as she is walking home on a dark street and forced into a car by several men is usually too frightened to resist, and if she does, her efforts are more likely to result in injury than escape from her fate. The young woman at a drinking party who remains after the other girls have left may find that the men take advantage of the situation.

The victim may be seized by several men when she leaves a tavern, or she may be taken into a back room and raped. Sometimes two or three women who are together will be offered a ride home. One woman, two if there are three women, will be driven to their homes, but the last woman will be driven to a suitable location and raped.

A not infrequent pattern is for a man who has had prior sexual relations with a girl to set her up for rape by some of his friends. The man invites the girl to a party. On arrival she finds that no other girls are present and if she expresses concern, she will be told that others are expected to arrive shortly. After some drinking she is forcibly raped by all present except her boyfriend. His companions go through the motions of threatening him with a gun to prevent his intervention on behalf of the girl, who usually has no idea of his role in the group rape. She is threatened with bodily injury or death if she reports the rape to the police.

Fraternity groups and members of football, baseball, or other athletic groups sometimes become involved in group rapes. Camille Paglia warns that a woman going to a fraternity party is walking into Testosterone Flats, full of prickly cacti and blazing guns. High school students or a neighborhood group of adolescents may also join together and rape a girl they know. The rape may or may not be planned in advance. Drinking and drug use often contribute to the crime. Members of the group not sharing enthusiasm for the project, nevertheless take part, because they lack self-confidence and fear intimidation or ridicule.

Nathan McCall, author of *Makes Me Wanna Holler: A Young Black Man in America,* provides a moving account of his distress at the age of fourteen, when faced with the decision of whether to participate in the group rape of a terrified, thirteen-year-old girl. He described her as cupping her hands over her eyes, as if she was hiding from a bad scene in a horror movie. When told it was his turn, he faked intercourse by pretending to grind hard for a few miserable minutes.

"I got up and signalled for the next man to take his turn. While straightening my pants, I walked over to a corner where two or three dudes stood, grinning proudly. Somebody whispered, 'That shit is *good,* ain't it?' I said 'Yeah, man that shit is good.' Actually I felt sick and unclean."

The Spur Posse

The Spur Posse, a group of high school athletes in Lakewood, California attracted national attention in March 1993 when eight members were arrested on suspicion of offenses that included unlawful intercourse and rape. Seven girls, age ten to sixteen, said they had been sexually assaulted by members of the group. The youths were released and prosecutors charged only one youth for having sex with a ten-year-old girl.

Posse members scored a point each time they had sex with a different girl. The top scorer had 66 points. Some girls complained that they agreed to have sex with one member of the posse and were then intimidated into having sex with other members of the group.

A sixteen-year-old girl told the sheriff's department that a Spur had removed her clothes in a park during a sexual encounter, then refused to give them back until she had sex with other Spurs. She said her clothing was returned only after she screamed. She believes the commotion prevented a gang rape (Smolowe).

Some Posse members boasted about their exploits and their parents defended them. Smolowe quotes comments of fathers: "Nothing my boy did was anything any red-blooded American boy wouldn't do at his age" and "I'm forty. We used to talk about scoring in my high school, what's the difference?"

Blame was placed on the victims. One father said the girls "were giving it away." A mother said the girls were trash. Posse members were cheered when they returned to classes.

Group Sex Can Be Dangerous

The pleasure of the act of love is gross and brief, and brings loathing after it.

Petronious, *Fragments.*

Women seldom seek out, or agree to sex involving more than two men. Occasionally young girls will actively participate in group sex. A girl meets three or four youths in a movie theater, games arcade, or shopping mall and agrees to go with them in their car. Within a short time she is giving them oral sex as the car is driven down the highway. The youths want their friends to share in their windfall. They go to the home of one youth and friends are invited over. The party gets noisy and they are asked to leave.

As they are driving away the girl suggests vaginal sex. She says she is in her period, and then she says she was just kidding. She starts ordering them around and lists the order in which she will take them on. The youth who wanted to be the first is told that he will have to wait. A decision that displeases him very greatly. The first man to have sex discovers she is in her period. The driver says, "I don't want her messing up my car, get her out of the car." He is concerned about his new lambskin seat covers.

The driver orders her out of the car. She refuses to leave so he pulls her out and her head hits the pavement. The youth, who was told he would not be first, kicks her. A passenger in one of the other cars punches her. He has not forgotten her telling him in front of his friends that he had a small dick, when she gave him oral sex. Left alone and bleeding alongside a park she goes to a home and asks that someone call the police.

She cries rape by nine to ten high school students. She was not raped but she was physically assaulted by three or four disgruntled members of the group. Both youths and adults involved in group sex with a promiscuous female lose any respect they may have had for her and often some turn on their benefactor, sometimes beating her severely.

GANG RAPE

Company, villainous company, hath been the spoil of me.

Shakespeare, *Henry IV*

"Gang bangs" or "trains" are a feature of the social life of street gangs in the larger cities. Often a girl with a reputation for promiscuity is selected. Members of motorcycle gangs are much older than members of street gangs, but they also select women of doubtful reputation who are drinking in their clubhouse or have gone on a ride. Some girlfriends of gang members do not always appreciate that willingness to have sex with one gang member is sometimes regarded as willingness to have sex with all members. Motorcycle gang rapes seldom result in rape convictions.

Youth gang initiations may involve rape. A girl who wants to join a gang finds that the initiation ceremony involves sex with all male members of the gang. There may be no advance notice. The girls are given alcohol or drugs before they are held down and raped. Some of the girls consider the gang rape a badge of honor. They want to belong to the gang and the initiation proves that they have what it takes to be members.

A youth who wants to join a gang may find that two girls are invited to the initiation ceremony and are supplied with marihuana and alcohol.

By the time the girls are in an advanced stage of intoxication, all members of the gang rape them. In many street gangs, rape is not a feature of the gangs' activities. Individual members may take advantage of promiscuous girls who are very drunk.

REFERENCES

Amiel, Barbara.: Men and their natural sexuality on trial. *Sunday Times.* (London), December 15, 1991.

Gilbert, Neil.: The campus rape scare. *Wall Street Journal,* June 27, 1991.

Kanin, E.J. Date rape. *Victimology, 9:*95, 1984.

Koss, M.P.: Defending date rape. *J Interpersonal Violence 7:*122, 1992.

Koss, M.P., Gidycz, C.A., and Wisniewski, N.: The scope of rape: Incidence and prevalence of sexual aggression and victimization in a national sample higher education students. *J Consult Clin Psychol, 55:*162, 1987.

Koss, M. P., and Harvey, M. R.: *The Rape Victim.* Stephen Greene Press, 1987.

McCall, Nathan.: *Makes Me Wanna Holler: A Young Black Man in America.* New York, Random House, 1994.

Muehlenhard, C.L. and Hollabaugh, L.C.: Do women sometimes say no when they mean yes? *J Personality Social Psychol 54:* 872,1988.

Paglia, Camille.: *Sex, Art, and American Culture.* New York, Vintage Books, 1992.

Parrot, Andrea and Bechhofer, Laurie.: *Acquaintance Rape: The hidden crime.* New York, John Wiley, 1991.

Sarler, Carol.: Putting the case against rape. *Sunday Times,* (London). February 2, 1992.

Smolowe, Jill.: Sex with a scorecard. *Time,* April 5, 1993.

Warsaw, Robin.: *I Never Called it Rape; The Ms. Report on Recognizing, Fighting, and surviving Date and Acquaintance Rape.* New York, Harper and Row, 1988.

Chapter 4

HOMICIDE AND RAPE:
A Monstrous Crime

*Murder most foul, as in the best it is: But this most foul,
strange and unnatural.*

Shakespeare, *Hamlet*

Rapists seldom murder their victims. It is difficult to obtain statistics on rape-murders, as the offenders are usually charged with murder and the associated rape may not be listed in crime statistics. Force used to subdue the woman may result in death, although this outcome may not have been intended by the assailant. The offender, either deliberately or in panic, may kill in order to avoid detection. Serial sex murderers kill again and again, but they spare the lives of some victims.

The woman who makes scathing comments on the small size of a man's penis, complains about his impotence, or ridicules his sexual performance, may be quite surprised by his fury. Indeed, she may never again have the opportunity to express her opinion on any subject. Rapists with great anger toward the victim, or toward many women, may start with rape in mind but end with murder. The sadistic murderer, once having tasted blood, is likely to kill again.

A SADISTIC SEXUAL MURDERER

The rape offender who is the greatest danger to women is the sadistic sexual murderer. A prime example is Peter Kurten, the Monster of Dusseldorf. He gained sexual excitement from killing women, men, children, and animals. At the age of thirteen, Kurten first became aware of the connection between cruelty and sex when he became sexually aroused while stabbing sheep. At fourteen he ejaculated while strangling a squirrel. He also ejaculated watching big fires and he had an orgasm looking at blood gush from a man run over by a streetcar.

His wife complained about his lack of interest in sex and she usually took the initiative. She had to help him get an erection and he could not maintain it unless he had fantasies of violence. With other women he was unable to perform sexually without ill-treating the woman or resorting to cutting, stabbing, or striking with a hammer. He ejaculated on sucking the blood of mortally wounded victims. Kurten told Karl Berg, M.D., the Medico-Legal Officer of the Dusseldorf Criminal Court, that if he had the means he would have killed masses. He described his feelings following his crimes: "Sometimes when I seized my victim's throat, I had an orgasm; sometimes not, but then the orgasm came as I stabbed the victim. It was not my intention to get satisfaction by normal intercourse, but by killing. When the victim struggled she merely stimulated my lust... That I wasn't out for normal sexual enjoyment you can tell from the Scheer case. That was a man... The man was staggering. He bumped into me. He was drunk. I stabbed him with the scissors. At the first stab in the temple he fell down. Then at once I got sexual excitement, and the more I stabbed the more intense it became. I gave him a severe stab in the neck and I heard distinctly the faint gushing of his blood. That was the climax. Then came the ejaculation. I stopped stabbing and just rolled the body over the bank" (Berg).

Kurten murdered or attempted to murder over forty persons. At the age of nine he drowned two playmates in the Rhine. His first murder as an adult was committed at the age of thirty in a burglary. Like some other serial murderers, he varied his methods of killing—strangling, stabbing and assault with a blunt instrument—to convince the police that several murderers were responsible for his crimes. Some victims were raped. He derived considerable satisfaction from the newspaper publicity given to his crimes and he wrote letters in disguised handwriting to the press and to the police giving them information about his murders. He liked to return to the graves of his victims.

In his childhood, as well as in adult life, he was a firesetter and was cruel to both children and animals. He set fire to haystacks, buildings and a forest. Gasoline was used to burn the body of one victim. There were at least twenty-two fires as well as attempts to burn an orphanage. His sadistic behavior may well have been the result of his childhood experiences of brutality in relation to sex.

He was afraid of his brutal, alcoholic incestuous father and would often hide from him. His father's wages were spent on drinking and the family lived in poverty. "We all lived in one room. You will appreciate what effect that had on me sexually." He observed his parents having sexual relations and commented, "When I look back and think of the married life of my parents today I really think that had they not been married one would have had to think of it as rape" (Berg). His father was sentenced to eighteen months in prison for incest with his eldest daughter.

In 1931, at the age of forty-eight, Peter Kurten was found guilty of nine murders as well as seven attempted murders and was sentenced to death. He wondered about his execution and asked Doctor Berg whether, with his head chopped off, he would still hear the gushing of blood. This would be for him, he said, the pleasure of all pleasures.

RAPE AFTER MURDER

"If I killed them, you know, they couldn't reject me as a man. It was more or less making a doll of a human being."

Edmund E. Kemper III

Edmund Kemper is an excellent—perhaps deplorable would be a better word—example of a necrophiliac who killed women in order to have sexual relations with them. There were warning signs in his youth that all was not well. He cut off the heads and hands of a sister's doll, he cut off the head of the family cat, and killed neighborhood dogs. A sister who thought he liked a second grade teacher suggested that he kiss her and he replied that he would have to kill her first. He would stage his own execution in which he had his younger sister lead him to a chair, blindfold him, and pull an imaginary lever, after which he would writhe about as if dying in a gas chamber (Lundee).

In 1964, at the age of fifteen, he was sent to live with his paternal grandparents. He thought his grandmother was bossy like his mother and had fantasies of killing her. When she told him not to shoot birds he shot and stabbed her, shot his grandfather, then telephoned his mother to tell her they were dead. After his arrest he regretted that he had not taken the opportunity to undress his grandmother. During his five years confinement at the Atascadero State Hospital, he learned that the real target of his homicidal anger was his mother rather than his grandmother.

Kemper was able to obtain employment with the California State Highway Department but he continued to have difficulty getting along with his mother. Although six feet nine inches tall with very superior intelligence (IQ 136), he lacked confidence in himself and felt inadequate around women. He did have sexual relations once with one woman, but she refused to have anything further to do with him. Ed began to offer rides to university student hitchhikers but resented the superior attitude of these students. There were thoughts of raping them, but first he had to kill them. "I had fantasies about mass murder, whole groups of select women I could get together in one place, get them dead and then make mad passionate love to their dead corpses. Taking life away from them, a living human being, and then having possession of everything that used to be theirs. All that would be mine. Everything" (Cheney).

Between May 1972 and February 1973 he killed six students. It embarrassed him that while handcuffing one victim, the back of his hand brushed against one of her breasts and he apologized. The girls were strangled, stabbed, or shot, then taken to his apartment or his mother's apartment. A body would be hidden in a closet and when mother left for work the next day he would have sexual intercourse. There was oral as well as vaginal sex with some victims. He said he cut their heads off to delay identification but it gave him a sexual thrill. One head was buried in his mother's garden facing his room so he could talk to it.

In April 1973, he killed his mother by hitting her with a hammer and cutting her throat. He used her head as a dart board and flushed her larynx down the garbage disposal. It was reported that he sexually assaulted his mother's corpse. An elderly friend of his mother was also killed. A full account of his crimes is provided by Margaret Cheney in *The Coed Killer.*

After the last two homicides, he drove to Pueblo, Colorado where he telephoned the Santa Cruz police to confess his crimes. The Pueblo police who arrested him found in his car a 12 gauge shotgun loaded with three rounds, a .30 caliber carbine rifle loaded with thirty rounds, a .3006 caliber rifle loaded with five rounds, a cartridge belt with 100 rounds and additional ammunition. He said he wanted to turn himself in before he did something like shooting innocent people that he might happen to pass by. He was sentenced to life in prison.

AN IMPULSIVE RAPE–MURDER

A twenty-five-year-old man who was not on speaking terms with his wife spent Saturday afternoon drinking with a buddy. He had been feeling depressed that day because of a quarrel with his wife. During the evening he returned home to obtain his rifle, but exchanged no words with his wife. After visiting several bars he drove to a lake where he swam for about an hour. After this he shot one or two rabbits that were caught in the lights of his car. He drove around aimlessly and finally drove alongside a dam. On a sudden impulse he shot at the headlights, tires and windows of a car which was parked there. "I guess I was angry, I can't remember now what it was. It wasn't exactly anger, I kind of felt tense." He did not think there was anyone in the car and he was surprised to find two young couples huddled inside.

At gunpoint he robbed the men of their wallets; and as he feared they might attack him while he was turning his car around, he decided to take one of the girls as a hostage. The girl he chose, a slim attractive blonde, on his instruction drove his car farther into the mountains. After about forty-five minutes they were forced to stop because of a flat tire. He then raped her. While he was changing the tire, the girl ran down the road which was illuminated by the headlights.

"I hollered at her to stop. She didn't, I panicked, got scared or something, I fired twice. With a rifle I'm an expert, I aimed right at her head—her blonde hair showed out better than anything else—that's what I shot at. I wanted to stop her, I didn't want her to run away. I went out, she was kind of kicking, one of her legs was moving, I shot her again. I felt her pulse. If I felt it once, I felt it a dozen times. I must have killed her instantly. I knew I had to hide her then. As far as thinking about the law, I wasn't thinking about the law; I never thought about the consequences till it was all over. I've imagined that this is all a bad dream. I knew I done this, but I can't make myself believe I did it."

After burying the body some eight hundred feet up a steep slope in the mountains, he remained there for three or four hours wondering what he should do. He then drove to Wyoming, where he decided to return to his home in Colorado and "get it over." He realized, correctly, that his car would be traced, and he was arrested the following day. Within thirty minutes he confessed the crime and later he led the officers to the burial spot, since he thought his victim deserved a decent burial.

On psychiatric examination he cooperated readily. He appeared depressed over his situation and expressed considerable remorse for his crime.

A rather taciturn man, he described himself as a person who preferred to get on with the job rather than talk about it. "I never speak my opinion on anything. I just go along with the crowd. I'm not one to judge other people. What other people do is their business. It's hard to get me mad; I seldom argue." Review of his personal history revealed that he was smaller than other children of his age and this always made him "feel out of place." He complained that the older school children used to pick on him. At ten years of age he became very friendly with a blonde girl; they always liked to do things together. It was agreed some years later that they would marry when they were old enough. At the age of seventeen he returned home after a week's absence to learn that his girl friend had married another man. At first he could not believe the news and when he realized it was true he became very angry. "I could have strangled her at the time, I really got mad at her. After she jilted me, I didn't have anything to do with blonde girls."

A year later he married a girl who was about the complete opposite of his former girl friend in appearance and character. The marriage was not a success. There were three children of the marriage. Since his wife did not want any more children, he underwent a sterilization operation. Although he denied any regrets about this operation, the psychological effects of this operation may have been of some importance.

Although he blamed himself for the failure of the marriage, he complained that his wife was moody and sexually cold. There had been no sexual relations for the three months preceeding the tragedy. They seldom argued, but for periods of up to a week at a time they would hardly exchange a word. Following one argument he fired seven or eight shots at his mother-in-law's picture which was hanging on the wall of the living room. Following another argument he drove to the dam where he later abducted the girl and swallowed the contents of a bottle of his wife's sleeping tablets. He was discovered unconscious and rushed to a hospital.

It is significant that his victim closely resembled his former girl friend. He claimed that the resemblance did not occur to him until after his arrest. It is likely that his crime has unconscious determinants in his anger at his rejecting wife and his deep resentment toward his former childhood sweetheart. It is of interest that twice following arguments with his wife he drove to the same dam: the first time his hostile impulses were turned on himself in the form of a determined attempt at suicide;

the second time his anger found expression in shooting up an apparently unoccupied car and later in rape and murder.

He was found guilty of murder in the first degree and sentenced to life imprisonment.

A STUDY OF THIRTY–SIX MALE SEXUAL MURDERERS

Ressler, Burgess and Douglas have reported in *Sexual Homicide** the findings of specially trained FBI agents who interviewed thirty-six convicted sexual murderers. These men killed 109 victims, primarily women. Several offenders were suspected of additional murders. Only two of these murderers had no prior sexual assault conviction, and thirteen had four or more such convictions. Ten (28 percent) of the murderers were juveniles when they first murdered.

Sexual homicide was described as "Murders with evidence or observations that indicate that the murder was sexual in nature. These include: victim attire or lack of attire; exposure of the sexual parts of the victim's body; insertion of foreign objects into the victim's body cavities; evidence of sexual intercourse (oral, anal, vaginal); and evidence of substitute sexual activity, interest, or sadistic fantasy." . . .

Physical abuse was reported in the childhood histories for thirteen offenders. Twelve men (43 percent of the 28 men responding) reported sexual abuse prior to the age of thirteen. Nine men witnessed sexual violence in childhood. The childhood triad of cruelty to animals (36 percent of 28 men), firesetting (56 percent of 25 men), and enuresis (68 percent of 22 men) was well represented. Some data was not available on all subjects.

"An analysis of the relationship between sexual abuse in childhood and adolescence and sexual activities indicates that those sexually abused were (in order of magnitude of difference) more likely to engage in sexual contact with animals (40 percent versus 8 percent; p = .06), bondage sex (55 percent versus 23 percent), fetishism (83 percent versus 57 percent), obscene phone calls (36 percent versus 15 percent), indecent exposure (36 percent versus 21 percent), pornography (92 percent versus 79 percent), rubbing against others (27 percent versus 15 percent), and

---

*Reprinted with the permission of Lexington Books, an imprint of The Free Press, a Division of Simon & Schuster, Inc., from SEXUAL HOMICIDE: Patterns and Motives by Robert K. Ressler, Ann W. Burgess and John E. Douglas. Copyright 1988 by Lexington Books.

cross-dressing (18 percent versus 7 percent). There was little difference or no difference noted in the area of voyeurism."

"As adults, almost half of the offenders reported an aversion to sex. Sexual concerns and problems acknowledged in interviews predominated in more than three-quarters of the offenders. More than half described themselves as ignorant of sexual issues almost 70 percent felt sexually incompetent, 56 percent experienced sexual dysfunction, 30 percent expressed concern with genital size. Many were concerned with other sexual problems ('I don't think I'm like other people'); some men preferred sex only with dead women. The interviewers suspected that of the sixteen offenders who did not report an age for first consenting sex, most never experienced consenting 'normal' sex."

FEMALE SEXUAL MURDERERS

Rarely is a woman wicked, but when she is she surpasses the man.

Italian Proverb

Women, as well as men, gain sexual pleasure from torture and murder. A married man with numerous scars from cuts on his arms explained that before sex his wife would make him cut his arm. During intercourse she would become sexually excited by sucking blood from his wound. Karla Tucker, a prostitute, had an orgasm when she used a pickax as a weapon of murder in Houston, Texas in 1983. Aileen Wuornos, a hitch-hiking prostitute, killed at least seven men who gave her a ride on Florida highways.

Several women have assisted husbands or boyfriends in their acts of serial sexual murder. Susanne Hughes provided her husband, Philip Hughes, with the names of women who resembled a former girlfriend he felt like killing. Between 1972 and 1975 he killed three women who resembled her. To relieve his anxiety and tension and to sublimate his desires to kill other women, she submitted to sexual choking rituals with her husband. Susanne Hughes did more than submit to choking rituals, she also helped him dispose of the third victim's body.

Two victims were fifteen years of age and one was twenty-five. Susanne, who was granted immunity from prosecution in return for her testimony, said "Philip had control over me. I was sort of programmed to do certain things. The fact that I was going along with all these things he was doing to me, there had to be some sort of control because it wasn't anything I enjoyed, and I was afraid."

It is often assumed that the woman is an unwilling partner under the control of the male serial murderer. This was the viewpoint of detectives investigating three murders by twenty-seven-year-old Ian Brady and twenty-three-year-old Myra Hindley. There was evidence of abnormal sexual activity involving all three victims shortly before they died (Goodman).

During the investigation of the axe murder of a seventeen-year-old homosexual youth by Brady in Hindley's presence, the police were told Brady had claimed that he had killed three or four persons and the bodies were buried on the Pennine Moors. The police found a twelve-year-old-girl who had visited the moors with Brady and Hindley. She showed the police the area where she had been taken and a search revealed the grave of ten-year-old Lesley Ann Downey who had been missing since Christmas 1964.

Four days later the police found in the spine of Hindley's white prayer book, a souvenir of her first communion, and left luggage tickets for two suitcases stored at Manchester Central Railroad Station. In these suitcases were books on sadism and sexual perversion as well as photographs of Lesley Ann Downey showing her naked in obscene pornographic poses. There was also a frightening tape recording of this child screaming and pleading with Hindley and Brady not to undress her and to allow her to return home. There were repeated instructions by Hindley and Brady for the child to put something, possibly a gag, in her mouth. An additional indication of the sexual aspect of the attack on the child was that both adults had removed their clothing.

Other photographs showed Hindley and Brady posing on the moors. The police enlisted the aid of farmers, shepherds, and members of rambling and rock climbing clubs to identify the scenes, and within days each photograph had a twin photograph taken by the police. At the site of a photograph showing Myra Hindley holding a puppy, police discovered the grave of John Kilbride, a twelve-year-old boy who had disappeared in November 1963. The body was fully clothed, but the trousers and underpants were rolled down to the thighs indicating sexual interference (Goodman). Pathologists were unable to tell from the decomposed bodies how the children died, but they were probably strangled to death.

At first the police thought that Brady was the dominant partner, but their opinion changed during their interrogations. They were able to get Brady to reveal incriminating information, but Myra Hindley remained silent. As one detective commented, "She said nothing. No remorse. No compassion. No human feeling. Nothing." The only time she showed any reaction was when the Downey tape was played to her. She said she was ashamed. At the trial she gave her evidence in a flat, emotionless manner, declining her counsel's suggestion that a few tears would not go amiss (Melvern). Although she gave nothing away under cross-examination, she was found guilty of two murders and of being an accessory to a third murder. Brady was found guilty of three murders. Both were given life sentences.

Aileen Carol Wuornos: Serial Murderer

Like many male serial murderers, Aileen Wuornos used a con approach to persuade victims to go to an isolated place, then killed and robbed them. She would hitch a ride from older men by claiming that her car had broken down or her children were sick. Then she would offer sex. She claimed that the men became violent, tried to rape her, or did not pay her.

She gave various and sometimes conflicting explanations for shooting her first victim. For example, she said he didn't pay her, but she also said she thought he was going to try to take his money back. It does seem strange that a woman, who claimed to have had sex with thousands of men, would consider failure to pay for sex sufficient reason for murder.

She admitted shooting her first victim from outside the car, while he was sitting fully clothed behind the wheel. After she shot him he crawled out of the car and shut the door. She ran from her side of the car round to the driver's side, shot him again, and yet again after he fell to the ground. The victim was unarmed.

At her trial, the States Attorney, in his opening statement, reviewed evidence that would be presented to the jury . . . "She also told the deputy (sheriff) that she needed to kill him dead, not just shoot him because she didn't want to leave a witness . . . She said after all, I'm a professional road highway prostitute and if I didn't kill him, I couldn't go back out on the highway. They would find me . . . She said she intended to let him die" (Kennedy).

Her victims included: A fifty-one-year-old electronic repair shop owner, a forty-three-year-old heavy equipment operator, a forty-year-old former rodeo worker, a sixty-five-year-old missionary, a truck driver, a fifty-six-year-old child abuse investigator and former police chief, and a sixty-year-old retired police officer.

A driver in Florida, who picked up Wuornos on the highway, was offered sex: $100 in a motel, $75 in the woods alongside the highway and $30 for oral sex in his car. She said she preferred to go to the woods. That is where she killed at least seven older men "in self-defense." If she had to kill in self-defense in the woods, why did she prefer to go there?

Another man, who gave a ride to Wuornos and survived, was offered the best blow job he ever had in his life. He refused her offer not once but three times. After his third refusal, she reached for a comb in her purse, and he noticed a pistol. Quickly he pulled into a truck stop and gave her money so she could make a long distance call. As soon as she was out of the car he locked the door. As he drove away she threatened him, "I'll get you, you son-of-a-bitch. I'll kill you like I did the other sons of bitches" (Kennedy).

Male serial sexual murderers like to strangle or stab their victims. There are obvious advantages—dying can be prolonged, strangulation can be interrupted then resumed; selective stabbing of a bound victim can lead to a slow death. The female serial sexual murderer is at a physical disadvantage in overcoming men. Wuornos was about five feet six inches in height. A pistol changes the odds.

A small caliber pistol is not always as effective as one with a larger caliber, but perhaps there are advantages, one can disable a victim and prolong the act of murder. She used a .22 pistol. She shot one man over nine times, another man was shot six times, the last time to put him out of his misery. One wonders how long she waited before putting him out of his misery. Was it too late to call an ambulance? Clearly he was no longer a danger to her if he ever had been. Another man was shot while running away from her.

She would drive from the crime scene in the victim's vehicle. Like male serial murderers she kept trophies and she left few clues at the crime scenes. Fingerprint experts only obtained one print.

She was born on February 29, 1956. Her father hung himself while in jail on charges of kidnapping and rape. Her mother abandoned her when she was six months of age and she was raised by her grandparents. She said there was both childhood physical and sexual abuse, but later she denied the sexual abuse. At the age of nine she was severely burned in an accidental explosion. She became pregnant at thirteen after she was raped while hitchhiking. The baby was given up for adoption. She started using drugs in her youth.

At the age of twenty she married a seventy-year-old man. The marriage lasted one month. She said her husband beat her with a cane; he denied it and said that she beat him up (Edmiston). At twenty-two she shot herself in the abdomen in a suicide attempt. At twenty-five she was sentenced to three years for the armed robbery of a store. There were also arrests for forging two checks for over $5,000 and for carrying a concealed weapon.

After her arrest for murder, a former male companion said that she had once talked about a masochistic fantasy. While tied to a tree in a forest, a black hood would be placed over her head, a man would rape her and then kill her. She said the killing would make her climax (Kennedy). According to a film producer Wuornos admitted that she had a sadomasochistic relationship with at least one of her victims. She later denied this (MacNamara). She had a lesbian relationship with two women, one of whom she called her wife. In 1991, at the age of thirty-five, she was sentenced to death.

CHOICE OF VICTIMS

Serial rape murderers tend to choose adult females, often prostitutes but also women who attract the murderer or who arouse his anger; adult males, often prostitutes; young girls or young boys. They can change their preference. Rifkin, for example, after serving time, moved from boys to female prostitutes. Some kill men, women, and children.

REFERENCES

Berg, Karl: *The Sadist.* Authorized translation by Olga Illner and George Goodwin. London, Acorn Press, 1938.

Cheney, Margaret: *The Coed Killer.* New York, Walker and Company, 1976.

Edmiston, Susan: The first woman serial killer. *Glamor,* September 1991.

Goodman, Jonathan (Ed): *Trial of Ian Brady and Myra Hindley.* Newton Abbot, David and Charles, 1973.

Kennedy, Dolores with Robert Nolin: *On A Killing Day.* Chicago, Bonus Books, 1992.

Lundee, D.T.: *Murder and Madness.* San Francisco, San Francisco Book Company, 1976.

MacNamara, Mark: Kiss and Kill. *Vanity Fair,* September, 1991.

Melvern, Linda and Gillman, Peter: Behind the mask of a killer. *Sunday Times,* (London), April 18, 1982.

Ressler, R.K., Burgess, A.W. and Douglas, J.E.: *Sexual Homicide: Patterns and Motives.* Lexington Books, an imprint of the Free Press, A Division of Simon & Schuster, Inc. 1988.

Chapter 5

FALSE REPORTS OF RAPE:
A Very Sensitive Issue

The belief that all women are truthful and all men are
rapists does not prove us good feminists; quite the contrary.
It reveals us as prejudiced, narrow minded, and as bigoted
as any racist.

Angela Lambert

The imprisonment of a man falsely accused of rape was described in
Biblical times. Potiphar, a captain of Pharaoh's guard, employed
Joseph to take care of his household. Joseph was good-looking and
Potiphar's wife day after day kept trying to seduce him. Upset over his
refusal to go to bed with her, she cried rape. She told her husband that
when she screamed for help Joseph ran off leaving his cloak behind. Her
husband was furious and placed Joseph in the king's prison. Joseph
spent two years in prison before Pharaoh released him, because of his
ability to interpret dreams (*Genesis,* chapter 39).

Men still go to prison because of false claims of rape. Gary Dotson was
given a 25 to 50 year prison sentence for the rape of Cathleen Webb. She
became a Christian after Dotson had spent six years in prison and
decided to tell the truth. She faked the rape because she thought her
boyfriend might have made her pregnant.

"I ripped the buttons off my clothing, scratched my body with a piece
of broken glass, made a mark around my vaginal area and pinched and
bruised myself and did other things to make it appear that I had been
violently attacked" (Webb). Gary Dotson became a suspect because he
resembled the police artist's sketch based on her description of the
rapist.

The judge did not believe her retraction, but the Illinois governor
commuted Dotson's sentence to the six years he had already served.
Later, DNA testing, which was not developed at the time of the trial,

showed that semen found on Cathleen's underwear on the day she cried rape matched her boyfriend's semen (Dershowitz).

In Nebraska, Gary Nitsch, a 43-year-old married man, was arrested while shopping and jailed after Elizabeth Richardson accused him of rape. He lost his job and his children were taunted at school that their father was a rapist. Elizabeth Richardson testified under oath that Nitsch had raped her, but later admitted that she made the story up to get her husband's attention. She was charged with perjury and was sentenced to six months in jail.

FALSE REPORTS HANDICAP INVESTIGATION OF REAL RAPES

False reports drain police resources. Sex detectives, who should be trying to identify rapists and take them off the streets, have less time to accomplish these tasks. Patrol officers, crime scene detectives, and crime analysts also spend much fruitless time on false reports.

A 30-year-old woman who made two false reports of rape in Douglas County, Colorado pleaded no contest to a misdemeanor charge of false reporting. Under a plea bargain she was sentenced to two years probation and ordered to pay $10,000 restitution to the sheriff's department. The victim advocate who believed her story said that she had all the voluntary and involuntary reactions of a rape victim. The victim advocate even noticed the hair on the woman's arms standing up as she retold her story.

Weeks after her first rape report, a couple found her stumbling behind a recreation center. She seemed to have been bound, gagged, and blindfolded with duct tape. Her clothes were soaking wet. She said she had been raped again. But the story she told from her hospital bed was riddled with inconsistencies. Her father let detectives search his house, where his daughter had been living. In a waste basket, they found a pair of latex gloves and a role of duct tape. The tear pattern on the tape matched that on the strip used to bind the woman.

Captain Bill Walker, the investigator, wanted this case to send a message. "It's such an easy crime to falsely report and such a very difficult crime to disprove. A lot of other investigations went unworked because of this, and I don't think that's right (Ensslin)."

In Chicago, Tawana Brawley, a fifteen-year-old girl, who had been missing for four days was found huddled inside a plastic garbage bag.

She had been smeared with dog feces and racial epithets had been scrawled on her body. She told police investigators that she had been abducted and repeatedly raped by six white men, one of whom had a police-style badge.

Two citizens offered a $25,000 reward for information on the case, a boxing champion gave her a $30,000 watch, and a boxing promoter pledged $100,000 for her education. Some citizens charged that her attackers, especially if they were officials, would be protected and never prosecuted. Her advisers even claimed that an assistant district attorney had participated in the alleged assault against her. After a seven-month investigation, a grand jury concluded that Tawana Brawley had made up her story of abduction and rape, possibly to avoid punishment for staying out late.

The grand jury found no evidence of a cover-up by law enforcement officials and charged that Brawley's lawyers and advisers tried to keep authorities from learning the truth.

Self-Inflicted Injuries

The presence of physical injuries does not rule out the possibility of a false report. A 25-year-old housewife reported a brutal rape. She had injuries to her face, a bite mark on her left breast, rope burns on her hands and numerous bruises. Yet during a polygraph examination she admitted that she had made a false report, not only of rape but also of receiving obscene telephone calls and threatening letters. She ran face-first into a post to injure her face, bit her own breast and inflicted rope burns on her hands (McDowell and Hibler).

INCIDENCE OF FALSE REPORTS

Many rape counselors believe that women very rarely make false reports of rape. They become indignant when this issue is raised. A surprising number of psychologists, nurses, and social workers who do research on rape share the viewpoint that false reports seldom occur.

Eight percent of rapes and attempted rapes reported in the United States were unfounded in 1993 according to the FBI *Uniform Crime Reports.* Not all unfounded reports are false reports. For example, a report of rape to Denver police may be unfounded because investigation shows that the rape occurred outside the Denver city limits. The victim is referred to the police in the area where the offense took place.

In 1992, Buckley reported that police departments in seven Washington, DC area jurisdictions found that 439 of 1,824 rape reports, or 23.8 percent, in the previous two years were unfounded. In Denver, Colorado in 1990, there were 472 reports of forcible rape and 80 reports, or 16.9 percent, were unfounded. In the same year, there were 965 reports of aggravated robbery and 135 reports or 14 percent were unfounded. In most cities there are far more unfounded reports of rape than of other major crimes.

In an unusual study of 109 forcible rapes reported to a small midwestern police agency, Kanin found that 41 percent were false reports. No attempted rapes were included in this study. A report was not classified as false unless the complainant admitted that no rape had occurred. The police agency did not declare a rape charge as false, regardless of how much doubt the police had regarding the validity of the charge, unless the complainant admitted the charge was false.

The police agency was not inundated with serious felony cases and had the opportunity to thoroughly investigate all rape complaints. When a woman admits making a false report, it is the policy of the agency to charge her under the statute regarding false reporting of a felony. This offense is punishable by a fine or jail sentence. In no case, has an effort been made to retract the recantation.

Kanin also studied all forcible rape reports over a three-year period at two large Midwestern state universities and found that 50 percent of all forcible rape complaints were false. All reports and investigations were the responsibility of ranking female officers.

MOTIVES FOR FALSE REPORTS OF RAPE

There are many motives for false reports of rape, but most of them fall within the following classifications. The motives are listed in the order of frequency in the opinions of four experienced detectives in a sex crimes unit.

1. Alibi or excuse motives
2. Revenge or payback motives
3. Financial or other gain motives
4. Attention and sympathy motives

There may be more than one motive and the psychological basis for a false claim of rape may be much more complex than the woman realizes. Repressed erotic wishes or fantasies can be converted into beliefs and the woman may be convinced of the reality of her claim of rape as in the rare example of a middle-aged delusional woman who claimed that she had been raped over 200,000 times.

"They break in my apartment, knock me out, then bring other men in to rape me. They are doing this to make money. In Denver, Colorado, 65 percent of the whole town is raping me and bringing men from other towns and states to rape me for 18 and a half years. I need the money to get a twenty four hour police body guard to get this crime stopped."

Alibi or Excuse

A woman arrives home very late from work. She went to a party with a man from the office and stayed longer than she had intended. When her husband questions her, she claims that she was kidnapped and raped. He cannot understand why she did not call the police and suspects that she is lying. He may take her to the police building or insist that she call the police. When she talks to the detective she will make up a story about the rape, but may add, "I really don't want you to do anything about it." A false claim of rape provides an alibi in difficult circumstances.

Pregnancy

Pregnancy in an unmarried girl, in a woman who is divorced or separated from her husband, or in a married woman whose husband has had a vasectomy, was overseas, confined in a penitentiary or otherwise away from home at the time of conception is an awkward situation for which some explanation is desirable. A false claim of rape does much to maintain family harmony.

Venereal Disease

The married woman who contacts venereal disease from her lover may try to avoid detection of her infidelity by telling her husband that she had been raped. In order to convince him, she makes a false report of rape to the police.

"Loss" of Money or Jewelry

The wife who has paid for crack with the money intended for rent tells the police and her husband that she was kidnapped, raped, and robbed. A woman who reported that she was raped by a man who took her wedding ring admitted to a detective, "Yes, I've been selling myself for dope." Asked why she made the rape report, she said it was because she had sold her wedding ring to buy crack cocaine. The rape report explained both the disappearance of her wedding ring and her late return home.

Out Late and Curfew Violations

The girl who is required to be home by 11 P.M. but does not return until the early hours of the morning seeks to avoid punishment by claiming that she was kidnapped while walking home from her girlfriend's house and raped. She gives an elaborate description of her abduction by three men who stopped their car alongside her and offered her a ride. When she refused, two men jumped out, forced her into the car, drove her out of the city and raped her repeatedly.

She gets sympathy instead of punishment. "I lied; it didn't happen. I'd been out with some friends that my mother didn't like me to run around with. I got home so late I made up this story." Young girls questioned by police for curfew violations may claim rape.

A Wrecked Car

When an eighteen-year-old girl stopped her car at a stop sign shortly after one o'clock in the morning, a man wearing a mask opened the passenger door and pointed a gun at her. He told her to drive toward the mountains. In the high country he forced her to pull over, then he raped her in the front seat. She was not sure whether she was penetrated by his penis or by his fingers.

He drove off and crashed into a cement embankment. Then he pulled her through the passenger side window and down to a river, where he pushed her in the water. She held her head under the water trying to appear dead and was dragged several yards by the current. When she lifted her head the man was gone. She hitched a ride with some truck drivers who took her to a Denver hospital. She told the police that the man kept his mask and gloves on at all times and she did not know his race.

The next day, after questioning by a detective, she admitted she made up the entire story because she had been drinking, was out after her parent's curfew, wrecked the car and did not know what to do. Her boyfriend had left the party with another girl. Her parents could not believe that she had lied.

That Guilty Feeling

False claims of rape are especially likely to occur when a girl feels guilty over having had sex with a boyfriend. If she has dirt on her clothing from sex on the ground, alcohol on her breath, or hickies on her neck, she may be fearful of questioning, and by her guilty look she invites what she fears, parental cross-examination. It has been said that the difference between a "good time" and a "rape" may hinge on whether the girl's parents were awake when she arrived home.

Discovery of blood-stained underclothing by the mother may also lead to false claims of rape. This can be rather awkward for the boyfriend, especially if the girl is under the legal age of consent, because even if the girl later admits she gave her consent, her boyfriend can still be charged with statutory rape.

Shifting the Blame—Guilt Over Voluntary Sexual Relations

A woman, possibly under the influence of alcohol at a party, agrees to have sex with a man. Later, feeling guilty about her behavior, she convinces herself that she was raped. Others at the party report that she was openly making sexual advances to the man. She admits that she consented to sexual relations.

Adolescent Runaways

Adolescents who have escaped from juvenile halls and mental hospitals report rape in the hope of avoiding return to their place of confinement. Some do it repeatedly. One girl made eight reports of rape to the police. On her eighth report she admitted she was on the run from a group home and would do anything to keep from going back there. While in a mental hospital, she accused four different men of sexually assaulting her. The hospital did not believe her accusations.

Traffic Offenders

Women stopped for a traffic offense, fearful of a charge of driving under the influence of alcohol, may attempt to distract the officer's attention by crying rape.

Child Neglect

If for any reason police are called to a home and discover the children alone, the mother, on arriving home, may claim that she went to a nearby store intending to return within a few minutes. She says she was kidnapped, taken to an unknown location, and raped. In fact, she was drinking in a tavern with a friend for over three hours.

Excuse for an Awkward Situation—Caught in the Act

Women who have suffered the embarrassment of being seen having sexual intercourse may later claim rape. A woman at a party could not find her husband and went to look for him. She checked their car and discovered her husband having intercourse in the back seat with another guest. The guest screamed that she had been raped, and the man was arrested. He proclaimed his innocence, but the woman told a convincing story of being dragged to the car and being threatened with death if she resisted. Later the woman admitted in the privacy of the detective's office that it was not rape. She became frightened when the man's wife started screaming and tried to attack her. "When his wife appeared I had to say something."

A fifteen-year-old girl and an eighteen-year-old youth had to stay after school for detention. After their detention they decided to "get it on" in the teachers' lounge. A security guard caught them with their pants down and they were both suspended from school for five days. The girl told her mother that when they started having sex she tried to push him off. Her mother insisted that she report a rape but she told the detective that the sex was with her consent and she never objected.

A rape report is especially likely to be made when a woman has been humiliated by onlookers. A woman was having intercourse with a professional football player. His hotel roommate awoke and started laughing when he realized what was going on. A drunk woman reported that she was walking through a housing project and stopped to urinate between two cars. When she pulled down her pants, two men dragged her to the side of a building where one man held her down while the other man raped her.

A witness reported that he saw her necking and later having sex with the man on the grass. She did not resist until she realized that a group of men were watching. Then she started saying "Don't Mike, don't." When the detective asked whether this was true, she said it could have been, but she just did not remember.

Revenge or Payback

Jealousy, a lover's quarrel, the failure of a client to pay a prostitute for services rendered, are among the revenge or payback motives. Probably the most frequent revenge situation occurs in domestic or date violence. A young couple have separated and the ex-husband comes to visit the children. The visit goes well and the couple have sex in her bedroom. Later there is an argument and he beats her. During the marriage she filed domestic violence complaints with the police but he would be released from jail the next day.

This time she calls the police, and just as they are about to leave she says, "Oh, by the way he raped me." She has bruises from the assault and has sperm in her vagina. The next day when she is interviewed by the detective she may have decided not to proceed with the rape charge and admits that consensual sex occurred before he beat her. If she persists in claiming rape there is the risk that her ex-husband will be charged with both rape and assault.

Lovers' Quarrel

A sixteen-year-old girl called the police to report that a man had forced her into his car and had taken her to a house where he raped her and forced her to remain with him for eleven hours. The following day she came to the detective bureau and said that she had not been raped. The assault consisted of light slap and she described the incident as "nothing other than a lovers' quarrel." She had been dating this man but had stopped seeing him. He persuaded her to enter his car after he saw her returning home late at night in the company of two other men, and they spent the night in his apartment.

Jealousy

> *The venom clamours of a jealous woman*
> *Poisons more deadly than a mad dog's tooth.*
>
> Shakespeare, *The Comedy of Errors*

A married woman brought her six-year-old daughter to the police department and reported that she had caught her husband attempting to rape the child. The father, who was asked to come to the detective bureau, said that he had never touched his child. While the detectives were questioning him, his wife called on the telephone and said that she had seen her husband with another woman. She was jealous and had made up the story of attempted rape.

A Woman Scorned

> *Heav'n has no rage like love to hatred turn'd,*
> *Nor hell a fury like a woman scorn'd.*

William Congreve, *The Morning Bride*

Resentment when a man breaks off a relationship may result in the woman telling police that he raped her. A woman reported that her former boyfriend came to her home, kidnapped her, drove her to his home and raped her. Kidnapping and rape are very serious charges. The man showed the detective a letter he had received from her asking that they get back together. He did not reply to the letter. Two days later she arrived at his home in a taxi with a bottle of champagne. They had sex, but when he refused to continue seeing her, she threatened to commit suicide. After calming her down, he drove her home.

The cab company had a trip ticket on the day of the alleged rape showing that the woman hired a cab to take her from her home to the home of her ex-boyfriend. She claimed that she had written the letter asking to get back together two months earlier and had not dated it. She said he had forged a recent date on the letter, but a handwriting expert said that she had written the date in the same ink as the rest of the letter.

If the woman becomes pregnant and the man loses interest in the relationship, a rape report may be made. A woman who reported rape said it had occurred once or twice a week over a period of nine months. She said that he had threatened her by saying he would bite her cheeks, put his hands on her neck or slap her if she did not continue to have intercourse with him. When asked why she had waited so long to report these crimes, she said that she was hurt and angry because he had told her if she became pregnant he would take care of her, but instead he went to California.

Male Insensitivity

Many false reports of rape are precipitated by a man's loss of interest in a woman immediately, or soon after intercourse. An eighteen-year-old girl who had sex with a man in his car called the police to report that she had been forced into the car at knife point and raped. The next day she admitted to detectives that she entered the car voluntarily and had sex of her own free will. She added "I got mad at him when he made me get out of his car and catch a bus. This was my reason for calling the police."

In a number of cases of false reports of rape the men accused have mentioned the woman's irritation over their poor sexual performance: "She got mad because I didn't satisfy her." It is possible that the woman interprets impotence, quick ejaculation, or failure to perform sexually as often as expected as an indication of lack of interest in her, rather than sexual failure beyond the partner's control.

Unreasonable Expectations

A woman told police that a man she met in a bar invited her to his home. During the four hours that she was in the house he raped her five times. At about 6:00 A.M. he drove her to her apartment building.

The next afternoon she encountered the suspect in the same bar and confronted him over what he had done to her. He was cold and unsympathetic. She was very upset and at this time she called the police. He admitted having sex with her five times. At about 5:00 A.M. she wanted to have sex one more time but he was so tired he got out of bed and curled up on some cushions. She got so mad at him that she dressed and left in her car.

Failure to Pay for Sex

A surprising number of false accusations of rape are made by prostitutes. Twenty minutes after a woman made a report of rape, she was arrested on the street for prostitution. She admitted that she made the report because the man did not pay her. A woman jumped out of a car, signalled to an approaching police car and cried rape. The driver told the police that he met her in a restaurant, and she agreed to sex in return for payment of her breakfast. Once they were in his car she wanted $50 and he did not agree. He had not had sex with her.

A woman reported three rapes in nine months. Each time her account of the rape changed as she was telling it. Each time she refused to sign her statement, refused to talk to the detective, refused to go to the hospital for a medical examination, and disappeared after making the report. The manager of her apartment house address said, "She's just a whore, you'll find her on the streets."

Most street whores like to have sex in a car or hotel room near the street corner where they pick up clients, so that they can continue their trade without delay. She was different; in each of her reports she accepted a ride from a stranger, went to their homes, and was raped. On each report she was unable to locate the street or address of her assailant, avoided eye contact with the officer, and smiled, smirked, or laughed about the rape.

Another prostitute who reported a rape and assault admitted that she had not been raped but had been beaten by her pimp. Yet another prostitute who reported a rape later said that the only reason she had done this was because she had been assaulted and dumped twice in a week and she wasn't going to put up with it anymore.

Some of the most dangerous serial rapists choose prostitutes as victims. When there is no independent evidence, the sadistic rapist, without any criminal record and a good reputation in the community, knows he is more likely to be believed by police officers, prosecutors, and jurors than a woman who is known to sell her body. Serial sexual murderers also know that the disappearance of a prostitute is not likely to arouse public concern. Relatives and friends may not go to the police to report her missing.

Other Causes of Resentment

One way of getting back at a brutal, drunken, or otherwise disliked father is through a false accusation of sexual assault. Young girls who are very attached to their fathers and distressed over the divorce of their parents may falsely accuse an unwelcome stepfather of rape. Presumably there is an underlying expectation that the accusation will lead to a reunion of the mother and father. In other cases the intention may be to separate mother from a drunken, cruel and overbearing stepfather.

A woman reported rape after she discovered that the man with whom she had voluntary sexual relations was not the film star he had claimed to be. A man who resembled the Australian actor in the film *Crocodile Dundee* arrived at a hotel in a stretch limousine. He picked up a young woman in the hotel and had sex with her in his room. She reported rape after she discovered that he had impersonated the film star. Men who have impersonated well known football players or other persons in the public eye, to aid in the seduction of women have also been accused of rape.

Rarely, a woman angry at the police officer who arrested her, may falsely accuse him of rape.

Financial or Other Gain

Free Medical Care

A woman reported that a man invited her to his apartment to have drinks. He told her to take off her clothes and when she refused, he removed her clothes forcefully and had intercourse in a manner described as aggressive. He told her that this was a one-night stand and he did not want a commitment. The man said that there was no rape. After a discussion, she admitted that she had agreed to have sex with him. She made the report because she wanted to have a medical exam to make sure that she did not have V.D. or AIDS and to obtain drugs to prevent pregnancy.

Legal Abortion

In those states which permit medical termination of pregnancy resulting from forcible rape, statutory rape, or incest, women may falsely claim rape to obtain an abortion. The state may require a certificate from the District Attorney stating that there is probable cause to believe that the alleged violation did occur.

In those states that permit abortions, a false claim of rape may be made, to avoid having to pay for the abortion.

Money from a Victim-Assistance Program

A false claim is made of both rape and robbery. The woman claims that her assailant took her rent money and asks the program to pay her rent.

A Ride Home

A woman dumped by her boy friend in a town several miles from her home claimed that she had been kidnapped in Denver, raped in the car and then pushed from the car in a nearby town. She was driven back to Denver in a police car. Later she admitted making a false report to avoid paying for a taxi.

Breaking a Lease

A woman, who had made prior false reports, wanted the police to confirm that she had been raped. She needed a copy of the police report to help her break the lease as she wanted to move out of the home where she was living. There were discrepancies in her account of the burglary and rape.

Parole Transfer

In one false report a friend of the complainant said she wanted her parole transferred out of the state of Colorado, and thought a rape report would help her.

Attempts to Discredit Police Officers

The owner of a tavern who is in danger of losing his license for serving alcohol to minors felt that he was being victimized by the officer who inspected his tavern for liquor code violations. In an attempt to have the officer removed from the department, he arranged for a prostitute to make false accusations of rape against him.

Attention and Sympathy

A fifteen-year-old girl said she was raped by the man who had raped her older sister. He told her, "I got your sister, now it's your turn." Eventually she admitted that she made the report to get the attention from her mother that her sister had received after she had been raped.

A sixteen-year-old girl, whose need for attention was so great that at times she would take the baby bottle from the one-year-old daughter of her foster mother, then go into a corner and drink from it, said she had been raped. Inconsistencies in her statements and the investigation resulted in classification of her report as unfounded.

A fourteen-year-old girl reported that a forty-year-old man forced her into his car, took her to a house, and raped her. Later she admitted that there was no rape; she wanted attention from her parents. Medical examination of a twelve-year-old girl who reported a rape showed no evidence of sexual intercourse. She admitted, "I made this up because my mother doesn't pay attention to me, neither does my dad. They're closer to my brother. He's five years old."

A woman felt neglected by her husband who held two jobs. She gave an elaborate but fictitious account of rape in her home in the early hours of the morning. Her ruse succeeded, as her husband gave up his night work.

Young women who have lost the affection of a boyfriend may attempt to regain it by a dramatic appeal for sympathy. Thus a girl calls her boyfriend in a distraught state claiming that she has been sexually assaulted and appealing to him for help in this crisis.

A young woman reported that while she was waiting for a traffic light to change, a man got into her car, pulled a knife, and forced her to slide across the seat. He drove a few blocks, then pulled her skirt up and her underwear down. He unzipped his pants and she could see that he already had a condom on. She fought him but he hit her in the face and raped her. When a detective interviewed her the next day, she said that she was mad at her boyfriend, who had just dumped her. She made up the story of the rape to make her boyfriend feel sorry for her. Married women threatened with divorce may also claim rape by a stranger.

CLUES TO FALSE REPORTS

An experienced detective can often predict that a complaint lacks basis simply from careful scrutiny of the patrol officer's report. There may be just one clue that arouses suspicion, but often there are many pointers. Even if the victim is uncooperative, refuses to permit a medical examination, fails to keep appointments, and reviews mug shots quickly without really looking at them, she may have been raped. No decision should be made until the victim, witnesses and, whenever possible, the suspect have been interviewed.

Even if there are inconsistencies in her statements and clear evidence of falsehood, the woman may indeed have been raped. For example, a rape victim, possibly fearful that she will be regarded as promiscuous, denies having invited the rapist into her home. In one such case the victim said that a man had driven her home from a tavern, but he did not come in her house. Later he broke in and attempted to rape her. She was able to escape to the street where she screamed for help.

Officers responding to an earlier report of a prowler in the neighborhood arrested the rapist in his underwear as he was hurrying to his car which was parked nearby. The officers, who took the attempted rape report in the victim's home, noticed two open cold cans of beer and a receipt with time and date on it for a six pack. The beer had been purchased a short time earlier.

On questioning, the victim acknowledged that she invited the suspect into her house, but when he made sexual overtures, she asked him to leave. Later he returned and broke in through a basement window. Police found distinctive shoe marks that matched the soles of the suspect's shoes in the dirt near this window.

A victim of date rape, fearful of pregnancy or venereal infection, drives to a hospital. Worried that her family and friends will criticize her for going to her date's apartment, she tells police that she was raped by a stranger who grabbed her as she was getting into a car in a parking lot. The detective wonders why the rapist did not force her into the car before raping her. She says that her clothing was torn off her but she does not have marks on her back from being held down on the asphalt.

On gentle questioning, she reports that she was seized by her date and forced to go to his bedroom where she was raped. Her date tells police that she agreed to sex which took place on the couch in the living room. A search warrant is obtained for her date's home. The buttons, broken off her blouse when it was ripped off her, are recovered from the floor of the bedroom. She was raped, but her initial false statement makes successful prosecution a real challenge for the district attorney.

The suspect is a prominent businessman and is represented by a defense attorney renowned for his success in the courtroom. It takes courage to resist the excuses for not prosecuting this case: to save the victim from the stress of a trial and the jury will never convict because she lied when she first talked to the police.

Lies

When the victim gives a false name, false telephone number, false home address and false business address the police begin to wonder about her credibility. A check is made to see if she has a police record. This shows that she has been arrested for providing false information to an officer. She tells the detective that she is from New York and has only been in Denver a short time. In the next breath she talks about all the years she has been doing dope in Denver.

Inconsistencies

In Statements by the Victim

The description of the rape by the victim to the detective differs significantly from her report to the patrol officer, and also from her statements to bystanders and to a nurse or doctor. In one case a woman who had been in treatment for multiple personality disorder later told her therapist that one of her personalities had agreed to have sex with the suspect.

Between Statements by the Victim and Witnesses

Persons who were with the victim prior to, during or after the alleged rape may provide information that contradicts information provided by the victim. Sometimes they are the first to raise the possibility or even probability of a false report.

A woman came out of a bedroom at a party, angrily complained that she had been raped by several guys and left. The hostess told police that the victim was "stoned." One of the guests told police that he was in the bedroom during the time of the alleged rapes. "I was sleeping on the floor. When I woke up I saw two people making love, so I just laid there. When the guy left the room, another guy came in and so they made love too, and it happened four times. By then I was not the only one who saw this and I went downstairs. When the girl came downstairs she said she was raped. She definitely was not raped."

Between Statements by the Victim and Suspect

A woman who had filed for divorce from her husband told police he had called her and asked her to meet him at a city park. After she got in his car he forced her in the back seat and raped her. Before leaving he told her, "Don't bother telling anyone because I'm a police officer and I haven't left any evidence, so they can't prove anything."

She drove to a hospital. Extremely distraught and shaking apparently uncontrollably, she showed nurses scratches on her face, back, stomach, and inner thighs. Unknown to the victim, her husband a deputy sheriff, had just changed his regular hours of work and he was on duty in the jail section of the police building, many miles away from the city park at the time of the alleged rape. Witnesses confirmed that he did not leave the jail during the time that he was on duty.

Appearance

The victim says she was dragged through bushes but she does not look as if she has been dragged through bushes. Despite a vigorous fight, not a hair is out of place.

Medical Examination

The woman says she was beaten unconscious but she has no visible injuries. A drunk victim said the suspect threw her out of his car and drove over her legs twice, but a nurse could not find any injuries to her legs. She claimed that the suspect almost bit her nipples off, but there is no sign of injury. Bruises from alleged blows by the suspect are too old to have come from an assault the previous night.

A school girl claimed that six men raped her and that each man raped her six times orally, anally, and vaginally. A doctor reported that there was no trauma and no semen in the test smears.

Crime Scene

At the site of the alleged rape there are no footprints in mud or snow and no sign of a struggle. In a backyard where the rape occurred there is a fierce dog that was not mentioned by the complainant. The vacant house where the victim was assaulted is barricaded and there is no evidence of forced entry. The torn panties recovered at the scene had been cut with scissors or a sharp knife and have not been torn apart. Scrapings from the finger nails of the victim contain her own skin tissue from self-inflicted injuries.

Handwriting comparisons show that threatening notes sent to the victim were written by the victim. In one case of attempted sexual assault, a search of the suspect revealed a note written on a bar napkin: "How would you like some fantastic head, who cares where—just find us a bed." The suspect said the note had been given to him by the victim. On questioning, the victim acknowledged writing the note.

Improbable Events

Unlikely or improbable events speak for themselves. Truth may be stranger than fiction, but the claim of a robust young woman that she was raped by an unarmed middle-aged man in a wheel chair will test the credulity of even the most gullible police officer. A girl said that she had been held captive for eleven days and that in the first five days she was raped by fifty-five men. She said that she lost count after this, as many men came back for "seconds." Inquiry quickly established that she was a patient in a mental hospital.

One victim mentioned that two years prior to a recent rape she was chained up for three months by her boss and sexually assaulted during that time. She did not report this imprisonment and repeated rape. Another victim reported four rapes within seven months. Yet another victim said that she usually does not report her rapes since it happens to her so much, but this time she got a license number.

A woman said she was kidnapped in the lunch hour, driven up in the mountains, then raped. The man told her he wanted to keep her because she was "such a good fuck." He sat beside her drinking and smoking for a couple of hours before driving her back to Denver where he drove around aimlessly. Near her home she was able to jump out of his car. When asked where he had driven her she could not remember. He had driven for five hours but she could not remember where they had gone. He never once stopped at a traffic light, nor did he have to get gas, nor did he have to use a restroom after drinking beer for several hours.

A 200-pound victim claimed that the suspect carried her upstairs. Another victim said that a man on a date took her to a vacant home, assaulted her, then said he was going to cleanse her and painted her body with paint from a gallon can. A receipt for the paint later was found in the trunk of her car, and she admitted her falsehood.

A woman reported that a man dragged her into his car and told her that if she didn't suck his penis he would force her to suck the dog in the back seat. He ejaculated in her mouth and she bit his penis as hard as she could. The man slammed her head against the dash of the car, slugged her three times with his fist and threatened to kill her, but she was able to get out of the car.

She told the police officer that while she was a captain in the Army and a jump instructor for paratroopers, her parachute failed to open and she landed on top of a vehicle, breaking 161 bones. She said she had a steel plate in her head, a steel rod in her spine and plastic joints in her right hip, knee and ankle. She also said that she was four months pregnant and had an extensive malignant brain tumor. Doctors had told her she only had three months to live. Further investigation revealed that recent tests for pregnancy were negative and she refused to let the doctor check the injuries from the parachute accident. The Army reported that she had not served as a captain and had been discharged six years before the alleged parachute accident.

Puzzling Features

A young white girl is in all-black neighborhood without adequate explanation. The victim accepts a ride home from a stranger, yet she lives only three houses away from where she was given a ride.

Fierce Resistance, But Was It?

A young girl pushing her infant in a baby cart is forced by a much larger, older man to walk behind a building. He hits her, she kicks him in the groin and he runs off. It just does not ring true; why after taking the trouble to isolate her from people in the street does he give up so easily when she is so vulnerable with her small child? It could be her strong maternal instinct, but a subsequent interview without prior warning at her apartment suggested lack of concern for the welfare of her child.

Forced to Take Drugs

This does occur, but not as often as reports might indicate. A woman reports that she was forced to swallow four pills; or she was accosted by a man who got out of a car, grabbed her with one hand and put something in her mouth with the other hand; or she was grabbed by a man who held a cloth with a strange smell over her mouth.

The effects include immediate loss of consciousness or feeling light-headed, then losing consciousness and awakening while being led downstairs to a basement. Whoever heard of someone walking while unconscious, or of losing consciousness immediately after swallowing a pill, then regaining consciousness hours later? A cyanide pill acts quickly, but consciousness does not return.

Drunkenness

Drunk women have been raped, but a woman who is drunk may not be a reliable witness. A woman reported that she had been seized while going to the ladies room of a bar, dragged into a storage room, burned on her breasts and arms with a cigarette, and raped. The patrol officers took her to a hospital for a medical examination.

Later that evening the same officers received a call to the woman's home address. They found her in the middle of the street, very drunk, and nude from the waist up. Her boy friend was trying to cover her, but she proceeded to urinate in the street. She told the officers that she had burned herself on her breasts and arms with a cigarette earlier in the evening. There was no evidence of sexual assault.

Loss of Memory

Reports of partial loss of memory arouse suspicion. One runaway who made a false report claimed that the suspects placed something in her drink because she really couldn't remember much of what happened during the hours she spent with them in an apartment. Mild head injuries with loss of consciousness usually cause only brief loss of memory for the period after the injury.

Too Observant

The victim who makes a false report sometimes thinks that the more elaborate the report, the more likely it is to be believed. One victim seemed to be remarkably observant, describing many unusual features of the exterior of the suspects' car, yet she saw it only briefly. Despite spending fifteen minutes with the suspects, she felt unable to assist a police artist in drawing their faces. The victim who seems to have a fantastic memory may say so much that sooner or later she says something that arouses suspicion.

Too Unobservant

The inability to describe or identify a suspect observed for a long time always arouses suspicion. Despite spending many hours with two men who kidnapped her on a busy downtown street in daylight, then driving her up into the mountains and raping her, the victim was unable to say whether the men were black or hispanic. A young woman said she could not identify the suspects in a lineup even though she had traveled with them in two buses and spent many hours with them.

Failure to Escape Despite Opportunity to Do So

When an unarmed suspect stops at a gas station, fills the tank, and goes inside a booth to pay for the gas, why does the victim remain in the car? Even if he had a gun many women would flee.

Rape Is Reported Only after Woman Is Arrested

Adolescent runaways from group homes living on the street are often victims of rape, but sometimes they make false reports in the hope that they will not be returned to the group home. In such cases often a previous false report has been made under similar circumstances.

Prior False Reports

A rape victim advocate tried to find lodging for a transient who made a false report of rape, but no public agency was willing to take her. A psychiatric hospital said she had walked away, but the hospital did not want her back because she had accused all the doctors and staff workers of sexually assaulting her. A Samaritan shelter refused to take her for the same reason.

Delay in Making the Report

Although some victims are so upset over the rape or so fearful of the offender that they do not make a report or do so only after encouragement by others, nevertheless delay in making a report is often a feature of false reports of rape and other crimes.

Description of Two Identical Suspects

Sometimes women who make false reports describe two assailants who are identical in appearance. Often they are huge, 6 feet 2 inches in height and each weigh 260 pounds.

Bad News from Others

Discrete inquiries may reveal that relatives and employers think that the victim is dishonest or makes up stories. *Dishonest victims can be raped.*

Parents may volunteer that their daughter tells tall tales. One mother said her daughter had a flare for drama and would make up any story for attention. Whenever she has trouble in her life she reports some kind of personal injury or threatens suicide. The frequent suicide threats are accompanied by frequent change of therapists. As soon as a therapist realizes that she can't be believed, she starts seeing another therapist but does not mention that she has been in therapy before.

One mother said that her daughter ran with members of a street gang, sneaks boys into the house, and constantly lies. She has caught her in bed with boys. This does not mean that the girl has not been raped, but it shows the need for caution in evaluating the report of rape.

A victim's stepfather reported that she asked him to lie for her if the police called him. She asked him to say that she had not seen the suspect for almost a year prior to the rape. Interviews with friends of the victim may reveal that she spent the night with one of them on the night that she claimed she had been kidnapped and raped.

Injuries But . . .

The presence of injuries lends immediate credence to a report of rape, but the complainant may have injured herself. A girl said she cut herself on her arms "to make the report look good." The cuts usually are superficial and are on the front of the body, the cheeks, chest, abdomen, and thighs. There may be as many as 20 to 30 cuts or just one or two. McDowell and Hibler note that the wounds tend to be within reach, at unusual angles, and often conform to the range of motion of the person's arm or hands. The victims view their injuries with surprising nonchalance.

There may be crisscross lines, and occasionally words are printed. In one case the words were "I hate you." Handwriting experts thought the letters were written from the bottom up. Their neat appearance was inconsistent with the victim's explanation that she was struggling at the time.

Rarely the wounds are not superficial. One woman stabbed herself deeply in the back by placing the knife in the back of a chair and leaning back on it. She ran for help with the knife still in her back.

A 31-year-old woman found in bed naked, nonchalantly smoking a cigarette with her right breast amputated, told her parents that she had been attacked by a male intruder. Later she admitted amputating her own breast, which surgeons reattached. She admitted propositioning her landlord immediately before the amputation, but she did not link the amputation to her landlord's rejection. A diagnosis was made of paranoid schizophrenia (Coons et al.).

Victims who say that they were hit over the head and knocked unconscious may claim that they were unconscious for several hours but have no signs of physical injury.

Injuries from Other Causes

The victim may have been injured by others, but not by the alleged rapist. A rape victim with injuries from a severe beating told the doctor at the hospital emergency room that her pimp beat her. She also said that even if she had been raped it would do no good as she had sex with five men that night. Another woman claimed that she had been beaten, robbed, kidnapped and raped but her injuries resulted from a hit and run accident which she wished to conceal from the police.

She said she was about to drive away from a gas station when two men jumped in the car, one on each side of her, seized her purse and started going through it. When she screamed for help, they hit her in the face and chest. One man tore her slacks trying to pull them off and the other man grabbed her breasts. Curiously, no one at the gas station heard her screams or saw her vigorous resistance.

She was driven to a location, which she could not describe, and raped. The rapists forced her back in the car, drove off then slowed down and shoved her out of the car. She went to several nearby houses before someone let her in to telephone a friend who picked her up. She had blood all over the front of her clothing, cuts on her face, and damaged teeth. Curiously she did not notify the police until the next day, when the owner of the car she had been driving asked her why the police had not found the car. Only then did she report the rape. The police found the car a few blocks from where she made the telephone call for help. It appeared to have struck a tree and there was blood on the windshield and steering wheel from injuries to the driver.

REFERENCES

Buckley, Stephen.: Unfounded reports of rape confound area police investigators. *Washington Post*, June 27, 1992.

Coons, P.M. et al.: Self-amputation of the female breast. *Psychosomatics,* 27:667,1986.

Dershowitz, A.M.: *Contrary to Public Opinion.* New York, Pharos Books, 1992.

Ensslin, J.C.: *Rocky Mountain News,* November 23, 1992.

Kanin, E.J.: False rape allegations. *Arch Sex Beh.* 23:81, 1994.

McDowell, C.P. and Hibler, N.S.: False allegations. In Hazelwood, R.R. and Burgess, A.W.: *Practical Aspects of Rape Investigation.* New York, Elsevier, 1987.

Szurek, S.A.: Concerning the sexual disorders of parents and their children. *J. Nerv Ment Dis, 120:*369,1954.

Webb, C.C.: Trying to make it right. *People,* April 29, 1985.

Chapter 6

FALSE REPORTS AND FALSE MEMORIES OF CHILD SEXUAL ABUSE

About the worst thing that can happen to a child is to be sexually molested. About the worst thing that can happen to an adult is to be wrongly accused of committing such a heinous crime.

Margaret Carlson

FALSE REPORTS OF CHILD SEXUAL ABUSE

A substitute teacher in Chicago was cleared of sexual abuse charges after investigators uncovered a plot by a nine-year-old girl to frame him after he had sent some students to the office for disciplinary action. The girl had offered nine girls and one boy a dollar each if they said that the teacher had fondled them. Children quickly become aware of the power they have over adults through false accusations of sexual abuse.

A man was arrested after a twelve-year-old girl accused him of pulling her pants down and raping her in the home where she was employed as a babysitter. On questioning by the detective, the girl admitted that she had not told the truth. She was late returning home and her parents had gone to look for her.

After finding her they took her home and examined her underclothing. On finding blood in her panties, her parents became very angry and her father threatened to spank her. Because of a fear of spanking, she made up the story. Apparently her parents did not realize that this was her first menstruation.

A young girl at a drinking party with some college students fell down the stairs and injured her leg. It became necessary to call an ambulance. She was drunk and was afraid that she would be arrested for underage drinking. "Just tell them your dad molested you, they'll forget everything else." The next day she wrote a letter to the police saying that her statement about her father was not true. The Social Service Department had already been notified by the police.

These three examples are provided to illustrate the very real problem of false reports of sexual abuse of children. Some persons do not listen to the children, others believe any accusations the children make, no matter how absurd. Zealots believe all child reports of sex abuse within a family or day care center, but do not believe those children who deny that they have been sexually abused. We should always listen to the children and we should always investigate their reports of sexual abuse.

Social workers, psychologists, psychiatrists, and detectives should not use suggestive or coercive interviewing techniques.

The Anatomical Doll Controversy

There is disagreement on the use of anatomical dolls to facilitate interviews with young children. The presence of a doll house and dolls is less threatening to a child than a conventional office with a desk and chairs. It may be easier for a child to show what happened than to talk about it. Everson and Boat point out that the dolls can aid in focussing the child's attention, in a nonthreatening, nonleading manner, on sexual issues and body parts; convey tacit permission for the child to talk about or to demonstrate sexual knowledge and experiences; and may help to demonstrate that the interviewer is comfortable with the subject of sex. Many agree that dolls should be used only when other attempts to describe abuse have failed.

Experts who oppose the use of anatomical dolls point out that so-called anatomically correct dolls may not be anatomically correct and are provocative. The genitals are often oversized with open vaginas and open anuses. The child who inserts a finger into a doll's genitalia may be showing no more than a natural curiosity.

Ceci and Bruck state that it is impossible to make any firm judgments about children's abuse on the basis of their doll play because there are no normative data on nonabused children's doll play and no standardized procedures for their use (e.g., at which point in the interview they are introduced, whether they are introduced with their clothes on or off). These authors note that the data on anatomical dolls are equivocal.

"Some studies have shown clear differences between abused and nonabused children's interactions with the dolls. Some researchers claim that nonabused children rarely if ever show sexually explicit play with the dolls, whereas others argue that a small proportion do show such behaviors . . . Our reading of the literature suggests that the techniques for using anatomical dolls have not been developed to the level that they allow for a clear differentiation between abused and nonabused children. It seems that for a small number of nonabused children, the dolls are suggestive in that these children engage them in sexual play" (Ceci and Bruck).

In 1993, an interdisciplinary group of psychiatrists, psychologists, attorneys, researchers, and social workers from Europe, North America, and the Middle East studied the investigation of child sexual abuse allegations. Twenty participants signed a statement summarizing areas of agreement. The extract quoted below is from the section on using dolls and other props.

"The mere appearance of sexualized play with dolls should not ordinarily be used in and of itself to conclude that a child has been sexually abused. Instead, sexualized play with dolls may prompt a skillful interviewer to obtain more information, ideally using nonsuggestive verbal inquiries to supplement and clarify whatever nonverbal information was suggested by the child during his/her play with the props. Because defense attorneys frequently allege that dolls, especially anatomically detailed dolls, have been misused suggestively, we reiterate our recommendation that interviews should be videorecorded whenever possible. Courts and other potential users of investigative interviews should understand that there is no anatomically detailed doll *test* yielding conclusive scores quantifying the probability that a child has been sexually abused" (Lamb).

Physical Examination

Doctors, performing physical examinations, should not make hasty decisions based on a single physical sign which may be caused by factors other than sexual abuse.

In some areas, good clinical practice seems to have gone out the window; a sore bottom indicates sexual abuse; worms and monilia go untreated; and failure to thrive is insufficiently investigated. Molestation, preferably incestuous, is the fashionable diagnosis (Tylden).

Noting that, contrary to public belief, sexual abuse may leave few, if any, physical effects, the interdisciplinary group mentioned above point out that: "Even in the absence of physical signs, examiners cannot conclude that anal or vaginal penetration did not take place. Healing is extremely rapid, visible injury is not inevitable, and it is difficult to perform examinations on young children, making it more likely that minor damage will go unrecognized" (Lamb).

Factors Contributing to False Reports

Children make false accusations of sexual abuse, but many persons have difficulty accepting this, hence the "believe the children" campaign. Factors which contribute to false reports of childhood sexual abuse include: parental influence on children especially during divorce, child custody and child visiting disputes, children seeking revenge on one or both parents, children wanting attention, and children making false reports to divert attention from their own shortcomings.

There are adults who report recovery of lost memories of childhood sexual abuse. Do these memories come from the minds of their therapists, who see child abuse as a frequent cause of poor self-esteem, sexual problems, insatiable appetite, anxiety, and depression in adult life?

Incidence of False Reports of Sexual Abuse

In a study of 576 reports of child sex abuse made to the Denver Department of Social Services, Jones and McGraw found that most reports were reliable accounts, but 8 percent appeared to be fictitious. Acrimonious custody or visitation disputes were often connected with these fictitious allegations.

In a study of 1,249 cases of sexual abuse reported to child protection workers in North Carolina, the workers found that slightly less than 5 percent of the allegations were false (Everson and Boat).

Benedek and Shetky failed to document the charges of sexual abuse in ten of eighteen children evaluated during disputes over custody and visitation.

DAY CARE CENTER AND
NURSERY SCHOOL INVESTIGATIONS

A number of trials of persons who work in day care centers and nursery schools have lasted many months or even years at the cost of millions of dollars. Many of these trials have resulted in acquittals, but those falsely accused have suffered loss of reputation and loss of their life's earnings. Indeed many have been crippled by legal fees. Some of those convicted may have been innocent of the charges against them. Children coerced or bribed into giving testimony have also become victims of the criminal justice system.

McMartin Pre-school, California 1983–1990

On August 12, 1983 Judy Johnson told Manhattan Beach police that her son had been molested by a Mister Ray, who was later identified as Raymond Buckey, a teacher at the McMartin Pre-School.

"The boy, age 2½, had attended McMartin Pre-School fourteen times over three months and had been in Buckey's class no more than two afternoons. Johnson's complaints against Buckey grew increasingly bizarre. She accused him of sodomizing her son while he stuck the boy's head in a toilet, making him ride naked on a horse and tormenting him with an air tube. She made similar accusations against her estranged husband, an AWOL Marine, and three health club employees. Nevertheless, prosecutors presented Johnson as their first witness at a preliminary hearing in July 1984. In 1985, Johnson was found to be an acute paranoid schizophrenic; she died of alcohol-related liver disease in 1986" (Carlson).

Acting on the complaint of this mother and on a medical report that the child had been sodomized, the Manhattan Beach Police Department sent letters to the parents of all the children advising them that Ray Buckey was under investigation and inviting them to report any suspicions that their own children had been abused. The mass mailing, Chief Kuhlmeyer said later, "may not have been the best idea in the world. But we wanted to get the news out and we didn't have the resources to go down and knock at everybody's door" (Crewdson).

The letter requested the parents to keep the investigation confidential, but soon everybody knew about it, including Raymond Buckey and the other teachers. Parents were outraged and demanded prompt action by the police. The small police department lacked detectives trained in child sexual abuse investigations, relied on social workers to interview the children, and provided them with photographs and mug shots to show the children.

Social worker Kee MacFarlane, ill prepared for the task ahead of her, began to interview the children. Some told her that they had been raped and sodomized by Ray Buckey. Some said they had been tied up, drugged, and sexually abused by other teachers. There were also strange reports that children were forced to drink rabbits' blood and to dig up bodies in a cemetery. It was said that Buckey cut up the bodies with knives. Satanic rituals in an Episcopal church were suggested by accounts of men in black robes carrying black candles.

MacFarlane's interviewing techniques have been criticized. She was slow to realize that there might be more than one suspect. She rewarded children who reported abuse by the teachers and criticized children who did not. "What good are you? You must be dumb," she said to one child who knew nothing about the game *Naked Movie Star.* MacFarlane and other social workers interviewed 400 children and 350 said they had been abused.

On March 24, 1984, Raymond Buckey, his sister, mother, grandmother, and three McMartin teachers were arrested. It was not until October 1984 that the police chief requested help from the Los Angeles Sheriff's Department, which provided twenty-five sheriff's deputies under the command of a lieutenant. These officers began their investigation fifteen months after the initial report of sexual abuse at the McMartin school.

The Preliminary Hearing

The preliminary hearing, which usually takes a few days to a week, lasted for one year and eight months. There were seven defense lawyers, one for each defendant, and many child witnesses were cross-examined by all seven attorneys. A ten-year-old boy spent sixteen days on the witness stand. In January 1986, the judge ordered all seven defendants to stand trial. Ira Reiner, the newly elected District Attorney, dropped charges against five of the defendants because the evidence against them was weak. Raymond Buckey was denied bond and spent five years in jail awaiting trial. His mother spent almost two years in jail before she was released on bond.

The Trial

The two-year, nine-month trial of Raymond Buckey and his mother resulted in the acquittal of both defendants. In 1990, they were found not guilty of 52 criminal charges. The jury could not reach a verdict on thirteen charges against Raymond Buckey and these charges were not pursued.

Jurors reported that they felt the methods used to obtain the evidence were questionable. A major concern was that the questioning of the children had been too leading. Among other things, the children who admitted to abuse were rewarded, while those who did not were criticized. Although seven of the jurors believed that some abuse had taken place, they could not determine what portion of the children's testimony had been fact and what portion fancy.

The legal proceedings extended over a seven-year period and cost $15 million. Children were traumatized by days of cross-examination, especially in the preliminary hearing when they faced questioning by the seven attorneys who represented the seven defendants. In the words of the judge, "The case has poisoned everyone who had contact with it."

Wee Care Nursery School, New Jersey 1985–1994

The Wee Care Nursery School at Saint George's Episcopal Church in Maplewood, New Jersey employed five teachers and two assistants who provided services for fifty to sixty children, between three and five years of age. On April 30, 1985, one of the children on a routine check was examined by his pediatrician. While the nurse was taking the child's temperature rectally, he commented that his teacher did the same thing to him. When the nurse asked the child what teacher, he responded "Kelly." Although the pediatrician found no evidence of abuse, this comment by the child started the investigation at Wee Care.

Kelly Michaels had worked as a teacher at the nursery from September 1984 until April 1985 when she took a better paying job at another day care center. No complaints of abuse were made while she worked at the school. In June 1985, she was charged in a six-count indictment involving three boys. By December 1985, the number of counts had increased to 235 and involved thirty-one boys and girls. Her trial began in June 1987 and lasted nine months. The number of children in the indictment was reduced to twenty because some parents did not wish their children to be called as witnesses.

At the request of the investigators she took a lie detector test. The state's polygraph examiner reported that she passed the test. "At Michael's trial, the county prosecutors prevented the results of this polygraph from being admitted into evidence, basing their objection on a state law stipulating that any person submitting to a police lie-detector test must first sign an agreement authorizing future use of the results. Michaels, who had never before been brought into a police station, knew nothing of this requirement; nor did the detectives questioning her see fit to mention it" (Rabinowitz).

At the trial, the child whose comment in the doctor's office started the investigation, now aged six and a half, testified that Kelly put "gasoline" (Vaseline®) on the thermometer and then put it in his "bum," and she said nothing when he told her not to do it. He said that she also took the temperatures of two other children, and he saw her pull their pants down. Neither of these two children indicated that their temperatures were taken at the school. There was no medical evidence of sexual abuse to support the charges.

She was found guilty of thirty-one counts of sexual assault, thirty-eight counts of aggravated assault, and forty-four counts of endangering the welfare of children. She was not convicted of the anal penetration of the boy whose comment started the investigation. In August 1988, the judge sentenced Kelly Michaels, now twenty-six years of age, to forty-seven years in prison and $2,875 in fines payable to the Violent Crimes Compensation Board. She had to serve fourteen years before becoming eligible for parole.

In 1993, after five years in prison, her conviction was reversed by the Appellate Division of the Superior Court of New Jersey. The appellate court noted that:

"The accounts of sexual abuse obtained through interviews of the children ranged from relatively minor acts of touching to virtually incomprehensible heinous and bizarre acts. A common act alleged by both boy and girl students was that Kelly inserted knives forks and spoons into their 'butts,' penises, or vaginas. One girl said that Kelly inserted a light bulb in her vagina, and a boy claimed 'Legos' were inserted in his 'tushie.' The children told of games where both they and Kelly took off their clothes and, according to varying accounts, laid on each other, licked each other and Kelly, including applying and licking off peanut butter and or jelly, had 'intercourse' with Kelly while she apparently was having her menstrual period, defecated on the floor, ate 'pee and poop,' and performed cunnilingus on her.

"Kelly allegedly committed fellatio on some of the boys. Kelly was said to have played 'Jingle Bells' on the piano during many of these games. The acts were said to have occurred in the music or choir room, in the gym, lunch room, nap room, and bathroom. Kelly was said to have 'pooped and peed' on or in a piano bench, on the floor, on a lunch table, and made a cake out of poop that the children had to taste. She was also said to have taken her clothes off in the lunch room in the presence of both children and adults. Testing at the Federal Bureau of Investigation laboratories of a wooden spoon and piano benches for evidence proved negative.

"Several of the children claimed to have told their parents of Kelly's activities while they were happening, and some children claimed that Wee Care personnel were present or had been told of the occurrences. No adults corroborated the children's contemporaneous complaints. Many of the children asserted that Kelly threatened to harm their parents if they told of the activities" (625 Atlantic Reporter 2d Series. State v. Michaels 489 N.J. Super.A.D. 1993 West Publishing Company, St. Paul).

Rabinowitz mentions that one child told the court that Kelly forced him to push a sword into her rectum, then she told him to take it out. There was some discussion in court on whether the boy said sword or saw. Another boy told the court that Kelly threatened to turn him into a mouse and later turned him into a mouse for a little while during a plane trip to visit his grandmother.

The appellate court criticized the improper interview techniques of the investigators:

"The State concedes that many of the interviews reveal extremely leading and/or suggestive questioning. Certain questions planted sexual information in the children's minds and supplied the children with knowledge and vocabulary which might be considered inappropriate for children of their age group. Children were encouraged to help the police 'bust this case wide open.' Peer pressure and even threats of disclosing to other children that the child being questioned was uncooperative were used.

"A child was told that she needed to talk to help her friends and that the investigator had already spoken to five other children who revealed what happened. In some cases, certain children were told in detail what another child had disclosed. Sexualized discourse was encouraged and applauded . . .

"Children were told that they could keep Kelly locked in jail by cooperating; therefore they and their families would be safe. Anatomical dolls were used in the interviews, and in some cases the children did not disclose anything until they were either presented with the dolls, shown various eating utensils, or encouraged to demonstrate how Kelly *might* have hurt a little girl or boy.

"The records of the interviews show that these methods caused certain children to use their imagination and stray from reality, even to the dismay of investigators at times. In several instances, the children were tired and/or resistant to participating in the interviews, but the investigators continued to press for cooperation" (625 Atlantic Reporter, 2d Series. State v. Michaels 489 N.J. Super. A.D. 1993). The court recommended that a special hearing take place to determine whether the children's testimony resulted from suggestion and coercion.

The Appellate Court ruled that a psychologist's testimony that the conduct of the children was consistent with child sexual abuse should not have been admitted in evidence. The court noted that although a child may have been abused at some other time, this does not prove that the defendant abused the child. Furthermore, the behavior patterns of sexually abused children are not necessarily unique to sexually abused children.

The appellate court ruled that "The trial judge, in his zeal to make the children feel at ease so that their testimony might be obtained, failed to recognize that he could be perceived as crossing the line between an impartial judge and the prosecution. The judge in the televised-view of the jury, played ball with the children, held them on his lap and knee at times, whispered in their ears and had them do the same, and encouraged and complimented them . . .

"The judge also unduly interfered with defense counsel's cross-examination of the children and often took charge of the questioning, which in many instances was overly suggestive. For all appearances, the State's witnesses became the judge's witnesses. The atmosphere became such, after this manner of presentation of testimony from nineteen children, that a jury considering a verdict in favor of the defendant might feel that it was personally offending the judge. The required atmosphere of the bench's impartiality was lost in the trial" (625 Atlantic Reporter, 2d Series. State v. Michaels 489 N.J. Super. A.D. 1993).

"*Believe the children* is the battle cry of the child-abuse militants, who hold as an article of faith that a pederast lurks behind every door and blackboard. But child after child repeatedly said that Kelly Michaels had done nothing—and they had not been believed. The prosecutors had brought experts to court to testify that children denying abuse should not be believed. *Believe the children* apparently means—to those raising the rallying cry—believe the children *only* if they say they have been molested" (Rabinowitz).

ZEALOUS PEDIATRICIANS

In Cleveland county, England, within a five-month period, but mainly in May and June 1987 two pediatricians, Marietta Higgs and Geoffrey Wyatt, diagnosed sexual abuse in 121 children from fifty-seven families. The abuse included unlawful sexual intercourse with girls and anal assault of boys and girls. The doctors relied too much on the reflex anal dilation test. Indeed, in some children this test provided their only evidence of sexual abuse.

The anal dilation test has been described by Clare: "Part the buttocks gently in a normal child and the anus remains tightly closed. However, where there has been repeated anal penetration, the sphincter muscle relaxes and the anus opens as if in anticipation. The problem is that, as with all tests, there are limitations. Part the buttocks a little roughly, for example, and the anus may open. Persistent constipation, infection, anal fissures, can likewise affect the test outcome."

These doctors would waken, even after midnight, young children admitted to a general hospital for disorders unrelated to childhood sexual abuse. Over a period of several hours they would examine them and photograph their bottoms. Children, who had never been abused, were taken from their homes.

Nurses complained that the doctors very rarely came back to the ward to speak to the parents or the children once the diagnosis had been made and this caused a lot of problems to the nursing staff being unable to give vital information to the parents as to what was to happen.

One night the two doctors wanted to wake up a child who had not been admitted for sexual abuse in order to provide a control to compare the abused children. The nurses were upset at this incident and the fact that anal and vaginal examinations were taking place late at night. Nurses complained that whenever the two doctors diagnosed abuse they were elated (Report of the Inquiry into Child Abuse in Cleveland 1987).

Doctor Wyatt, in a telephone call, requested that an entire school of 120 children should be brought to his hospital before five o'clock that day for examination by him and other pediatricians. He wanted to know if this could be organized. Fortunately, the director of education decided that there would be no wholesale examination of pupils for alleged anal abuse within his authority (Stuart Bell).

Following a medical diagnosis of abuse, social workers would then question the children at length trying to get them to admit that there had been sexual abuse.

In one case a father was awakened by a social worker at 2:30 AM and told to take his twelve-year-old daughter and nine-year-old son to the hospital because the previous day Dr. Higgs had diagnosed his three-year-old daughter as being sexually abused. The couple separated. Later, neighborhood children teased the son for sleeping with his mother and the older daughter for sleeping with her father. They said they knew about it from hearing their parents talking about it (Oulton). Two weeks after Dr. Higgs made the diagnosis, the High Court ordered the children returned to their home, but the High Court could not restore the marriage, nor bring peace to the children.

Mary and Joseph Dixon, on the basis of an anal dilation test, were charged with molesting their daughter Vera. Then further test results suggested she had been molested on a car journey with her parents and two social workers, and finally on the basis of further test results, a foster care couple was also accused of sexually abusing her. It was months before the Dixons and the foster parents were cleared of the charges and the daughter was returned home.

The police soon lost confidence in these two pediatricians. The senior police surgeon considered their method of diagnosis of sexual abuse controversial and unreliable. Some of the children examined by Higgs and Wyatt had been sexually abused. An inquiry by Lord Justice Butler-Sloss did not reveal the number of children who had been abused. "The double victims of Cleveland were the most abused of all. In harrowing accounts . . . these children told of how having already been sexually assaulted, they were subjected to further distressing treatment by the doctors and social workers" (Clare).

CHILD CUSTODY DISPUTES

I have seen a few children who, when asked by examiners how they know the sex abuse occurred answered, "My mother told me it happened."

Richard Gardner

Wives involved in bitter divorce and child custody disputes have claimed falsely that their husbands have sexually abused one or more children of the marriage. The children are told repeatedly that they have been the victims of sexual assault and some may come to believe it. The moment a wife raises the issue of sexual abuse, judges tend to deny or restrict visitation rights. The husband has to defend himself and may be subjected to interviews by social workers and child psychiatrists or psychologists. The child may also be required to undergo evaluations by experts appointed by attorneys for both sides. The child who resents her father or stepfather may have her own motivations for making false accusations against him.

In false reports the child may reveal the abuse only after encouragement by her mother and then use adult rather than child-like terms to describe the abuse. One would not expect a five-year-old girl, describing oral sex by her father, to say "Daddy ejaculated." Rather one might expect "White stuff came out." One five-year-old child told Gardner, "I've been penetrated." When he asked her what penetrated means she replied "I don't know, my mommy told me I was penetrated" (Gardner, 1992).

The child who has been coached may blurt everything out very quickly. In contrast, the child who has been sexually abused finds it difficult to describe the acts and takes a long time to tell it all. False reports often contain little detailed information on the circumstances and nature of the sexual assaults.

The true victim is likely to be fearful in her father's presence, whereas the child who has been repeating mother's story may react positively or show guilty embarrassment over her betrayal. If the father has been gentle and seductive rather than abrupt and forceful, the child may react positively toward him. There is no single reliable test, but common sense and critical reasoning are helpful. It becomes more difficult to gain impressions when the child has been interviewed many times. This is why it is so important to videotape or keep an accurate detailed record of initial interviews.

FALSE MEMORIES OF SEXUAL ABUSE IN CHILDHOOD

If you are unable to remember any specific instances . . . but still have a feeling that something abusive happened to you, it probably did.

Ellen Bass and Lauren Davis, *The Courage to Heal: A Guide for Women Survivors of Child Sexual Abuse.*

In recent years much has been written about the long-term consequences of sexual abuse of children and it has been blamed for eating
disorders, poor self-esteem, depression, and a host of other common
complaints that have many other causes. Popular self-help books tell
readers that their physical and psychological complaints may have been
caused by childhood sexual abuse.

Psychotherapists, who suspect that their patients have been sexually
assaulted in childhood, may through suggestive, repeated, prolonged,
and coercive questioning obtain false childhood memories of sexual
abuse by parents, relatives, teachers, priests, or other persons.

The only way to tell whether these memories are true or false is
through corroborating information. Yet some therapists seldom speak to
the family or attempt to obtain information from others. They have a
duty to warn their clients of the need for verification of recovered
memories of childhood sexual abuse.

Recovered memory therapy may become less popular now that insurance companies are increasing the cost of malpractice insurance for
therapists. Within two years over 15,000 families have reported false
accusations of childhood sexual abuse to the False Memory Syndrome
(FMS) Foundation. The Foundation cannot judge the truth or falsity of
the reports that it receives. In the same period there have been over 400
recantations of accusations of childhood sexual abuse.

Some women have reported their newly acquired memories to the
news media, others have cut off relations with their parents, have sued or
sent their fathers or other persons to prison. Memories have been
recovered after intervals as long as twenty to forty years. Memories
have returned independent of psychotherapy. Something may trigger
recall, for example, marriage, the birth of a child, or some event that
has a link with the traumatic experience that was repressed. Repression
of memory has become a controversial concept about which there is
much disagreement.

Hypnosis and Sodium Amytal Interviews

Questions have been raised about memories recovered through the use
of hypnosis, or intravenous sodium amytal, a barbiturate drug. Use of
these techniques may make persons more likely to respond to suggestions,
and there is a heightened risk of recall of false memories. Some courts do
not permit information elicited under hypnosis to be introduced in

evidence. In any case of memories recovered through the use of hypnosis, sodium amytal, or psychotherapy, the memories recovered may be:

1. *True memories that had been repressed.* These memories may not be completely accurate. Always there is the need for verification of all major details of recovered memories.
2. *True memories that had never been forgotten.* For some reason the person takes the opportunity to simulate recovery of these memories. He takes advantage of the hypnosis, sodium amytal interview, or therapy to avoid responsibility for not revealing the information earlier.
3. *False memories that had been suggested by the interviewer.*
4. *False memories concocted by the person claiming recovery of these memories.*

An example of a true memory that had never been forgotten was provided by a man during a sodium amytal interview. He "recalled" the burial of a body in New Mexico, but he also provided false information. This man was arrested in Denver in possession of a stolen car. The trunk was bloodstained. The owner of the car had been missing from his home in California for some weeks and it was suspected that he had been murdered. The suspect claimed amnesia from the time he escaped from a California mental hospital two months previously until he found himself in a Denver hospital for treatment of a bullet wound received while trying to escape from the police.

During a sodium amytal interview he told me that he met the missing man after his escape from the hospital. One evening he left this man in the car while he went to buy some food. On his return he found the owner of the car with his head "bashed in." He was frightened that he would be blamed as he had a criminal record. He drove to an isolated spot in New Mexico where he buried the body, which was later found in the location he had described. This was not a recovery of a repressed memory. He knew where the body was buried. Later he confessed to committing the crime (Macdonald 1976).

Repression of Memory

Repression has been defined as the unconscious exclusion from consciousness of painful memories. Many psychiatrists and psychologists believe that repression can cause loss of memory of a very stressful experience. Yet such repression of memory rarely occurs because adult victims of violent crimes rarely have no memory of the crime. It may well be that few children repress all memory of a violent sexual assault.

A Three-Year-Old Child Remembers

In the following example, a three-year-old child was able to describe a very traumatic kidnapping, sexual assault, and attempted murder, which by good fortune she survived.

While playing in front of her home she was kidnapped by a man who was heard to tell her to take off her pants. She was driven to a remote mountain park fifteen miles west of Denver, sexually molested, and dropped ten feet down into the cesspit of an outdoor toilet. Three days later, hikers from Pennsylvania, who stopped at the outhouse, heard her faint cries. When asked what she was doing there the child replied, "I live here" and asked for something to drink. They telephoned for help.

The smallest man in the rescue team was lowered through the narrow inlet below the toilet seat, down to the bottom of the cesspit. The sewage was about one foot deep. The child, wearing only her underpants, was sitting on some sticks which she had gathered to form a ledge above the excrement. She grabbed her rescuer and would not let him go

Taken by helicopter to a hospital, she was found to have marked dehydration, bilateral "immersion foot," scratches and bruising on her back, bottom, and legs. Her sleep was restless and occasionally she would cry out unintelligibly.

She did not repress memory of the kidnapping and sexual assault. While still in the hospital, five days after being kidnapped, she was interviewed by police and from a group of photographs she identified the "bad man who put me in the hole."

Later she revealed to David Jones, a psychiatrist, that the "bad man," touched her vagina and had her touch his penis both during the drive to the mountain park and in the toilet where he made her sit on his lap. She described him pushing her down through the toilet seat. Jones considered that even though she was only three years old, she was able to relate accurately what had happened to her.

"She was shown the original photo line-up, but with the police suspect removed, and it was suggested that the series of eleven photographs contained the "bad man." She studied the photos in matter-of-fact fashion, then firmly stated that he was not among the photographs. After a snack she was shown the same series of photos but with the suspect placed at number seven in the series. This time, when she viewed the series and saw the suspect's photo, she startled backwards and gasped saying, "He want to put me in the hole ...he got a car." She appeared shocked and frightened" (Jones and Krugman).

Six and a half months after the kidnapping the girl gave a videotaped deposition for the court. Attorneys and the judge's representative, sitting behind a one-way glass, were able to suggest questions to Doctor Jones who had a microreceiver in one ear. She was not as spontaneous and did not provide as much information as she had previously provided on videotaped interviews at days fourteen and seventeen after the kidnapping. The court allowed all three videotaped interviews to be admitted into evidence (Jones).

Her account of the kidnapping and sexual assault was confirmed nine months after this deposition, by her assailant when he pleaded guilty to sexual assault and attempted murder. The twenty-two-year-old man, who was sentenced to ten years in prison, had a history of stealing women's panties, molesting small boys (fondling and oral sex), obscene telephone calls, and burglaries.

The Chowchilla School Bus Kidnapping

Lenore Terr interviewed a group of children who were kidnapped from a school bus, driven in darkened vans to a rock quarry, and then buried alive in a truck trailer lowered below ground level. These children were interviewed seven to thirteen months and again four to five years after the kidnapping. She also interviewed 153 children, five weeks and again fourteen months after the Challenger spacecraft blew up killing all on board. Terr comments in her book, *Unchained Memories:* "Every single child in both groups remembered what had happened. It is hard to repress striking events like those."

Yet Lenore Terr testified at the trial of George Franklin that his daughter Eileen had repressed all memory of witnessing her father's rape-murder of an eight year old friend. This memory returned when she was looking at her daughter twenty years after the murder. She also recalled that her father had threatened her life if she revealed the truth, and that her father had sexually abused her.

Controversial Viewpoints on Repression

Every man has reminiscences which he would not tell to everyone but only to his friends. He has other matters in his mind which he would not reveal even to his friends, but only to himself, and that in secret. But there are other things which a man is afraid to tell even to himself, and every decent man has a number of such things stored away in his mind.

Fyodor Dostoyevsky, *Notes from Underground*

Terr considers that memory of one traumatic event is not repressed, but memory is repressed when there is long-standing or repeated exposure to traumatic events. Many women have reported recovery of memories of many years of repeated childhood sexual assaults by their fathers. Would a child, who is sexually abused night after night for years by her father, be able to repress all memory of these hundreds of acts of sexual intercourse? This does seem rather unlikely. The child might well wish to rid herself of these disturbing memories. Just to think about the assaults is to experience them again. There may be a conscious decision to block out all memory of the sexual assaults.

Then one day the decision is made to tell others and perhaps eventually to confront father, to sue him, or to make a public statement. An explanation for the long silence becomes necessary. For those who cannot admit that they had no loss of memory, that it was something they did not allow themselves to think about, a claim of sudden recovery of (repressed) memories is made. The victim may herself believe that she never remembered the sexual assaults.

A victim revealed that from five until eighteen years of age she had been sexually assaulted by her father. All memory of the sexual assaults had been repressed until she was twenty-four. Her memory returned while she was talking to a minister of religion. She told correspondent Vickie Bane: "In order to survive, I split into a day child, who giggled and smiled, and a night child, who lay awake in a fetal position, only to be pried apart by my father. Until I was twenty-four, the day child had no conscious knowledge of the night child. During the day, no embarrassing or angry glances ever passed between my father and me. I had no rage toward him at all, because I had no conscious knowledge of what he was doing to me. Anyone who knew me would say I was the happiest child. I believed I was happy."

It is difficult to see how the day child does not know what happens at night. Is this a case of dissociation that takes place at nightfall day after day for many years? I am not questioning her report of repeated sexual assault. An older sister also revealed that she had been assaulted by her father.

Repression of one or two experiences is easier to comprehend than repression of assaults that continue month after month and year after year. The capacity for self-deception of the histrionic personality may account for some of the peculiar and puzzling clinical pictures. A woman conjures up false memories of sexual abuse in childhood to obtain the attention and sympathy she needs so desperately. Talk show hosts welcome her appearance on national TV. Her name is on every newspaper, but she was never sexually abused. Her parents have become victims of false accusations.

Another woman with a histrionic personality, who was sexually abused in childhood, succeeds for years in convincing herself that she was never sexually abused, but one day some unexpected stress overwhelms her and she has to deal with something she has avoided facing for all these years. Is it surprising if she claims prior loss of memory of the abuse?

If some of her statements do not match the memories of others, is it surprising that she changes her recall and gives a series of different accounts of events in the past and of the circumstances of her recall of the sexual abuse? She did not tell the truth when she claimed to have no memory of the assaults. She may have been inclined to gloss over the truth all her life. Histrionic personalities are not always reliable informants.

Memory loss is a prominent feature of multiple personality disorder which was formerly regarded as a rare disorder. Thigpen and Cleckley, authors of *The Three Faces of Eve,* a book on a multiple personality, have expressed concern about the recent claims of a high incidence of this disorder. In twenty-five years following publication of the book, the authors examined hundreds of patients who were thought to have this disorder, either by therapists or by the patients themselves, yet they have found only one patient with a genuine multiple personality.

They point out that many people who claim to have this disorder appear to be motivated (either consciously or unconsciously) by a desire to draw attention to themselves or to avoid responsibility for certain actions. Multiple personality disorder has been renamed dissociative identity disorder in the fourth edition of the *Diagnostic and Statistical Manual of the American Psychiatric Association.*

DSM–IV acknowledges that some mental health professionals believe that the syndrome has been over diagnosed in individuals who are highly suggestible. Many experts, however, question whether the multiple personality disorder, or dissociative identity disorder to use its new name, ever existed.

There are several causes of memory problems including infantile amnesia, repression, head injury, delirium, organic brain disease, too much alcohol, and simple forgetting. Loftus writes on the myth of repressed memories and there are many experts who challenge the existence of repression. Holmes after reviewing over sixty years of research could find no controlled laboratory evidence supporting the concept of repression. Is it possible to prove or disprove the concept of repression? How do you study scientifically an unconscious thought or an unconscious act?

The adult who recovers memories of childhood sexual abuse should think twice before cutting off all relations with her family. Vengeance is seldom an answer that brings peace of mind. The very thought of prosecuting or suing a parent in the courts should bring to mind an ancient Chinese curse to be reserved for your worst enemy: "May you become involved in a lawsuit, and may your cause be just."

ALLEGED SATANIC CULT RAPE AND MURDER

The Case of Paul Ingram

In September 1988, at a church-sponsored retreat intended to encourage women to reveal abuse, twenty-two-year-old Erika Ingram accused her father of having raped her when she was a child. In the weeks that followed, Erika expanded her allegations and reported that recently her father had been raping her nearly every night (Ofshe 1992). Julie,

Erika's eighteen-year-old sister, also reported rape. Their father, Paul Ingram, was the chief civil deputy of the sheriff's department in Thurston County, Washington.

Curiously, Paul Ingram, in the first interview with investigators, said that he could not remember having ever molested his daughters. He added, "If this did happen, we need to take care of it. I can't see myself doing this. If I did molest the girls, there must be a dark side of me that I don't know about" (Wright 1993). If he did not do it, why did he not say so unequivocally? Most fathers unfairly accused of incest would surely react with an immediate, angry denial.

As Wright notes, Ingram wasn't saying "I didn't do it"; he was saying he couldn't *see* himself doing it. By the end of the interview with the detectives, Ingram admitted to having sex with Ericka since she was five. He also admitted to having sex with Julie and arranging for her to have an abortion when she was fifteen.

Both daughters had previously alleged sexual advances by acquaintances. There were inconsistencies in Julie's report and Ericka's complaint did not justify charges. As the investigation of the accusations against their father proceeded, the sisters' accusations multiplied. The persons who had sexually assaulted them or had assisted in the assaults and the range of crimes came to include:

- Two friends of their father.
- The sister of one of these men.
- Their mother.
- Two brothers.
- Twelve members of the sheriff's department.
- Two police dogs who raped their mother.
- Hundreds of Satanic rituals.
- The satanic murder of twenty-five babies and one adult.
- Satanic rituals in which the sisters were tortured and burned.
- Abortions were performed on both sisters and the fetuses were cut up.

The detectives could not find any physical evidence. The daughters revealed where the bodies of the murdered infants had been buried, but a search for their bones was unsuccessful. Ericka later claimed that about 250 babies had been murdered.

Both Ericka and Julie reported that their bodies were covered with scars caused by the tortures they suffered. Julie could recall having nails driven through her flesh. For Julie, the scars were so embarrassing that she changed in private for gym class and wore a t-shirt over her bathing suit. After resisting for several months, both Ericka and Julie were court ordered to submit to physical examinations. The examinations revealed that neither carried scars consistent with the torture tales (Ofshe 1992).

Twelve members of the sheriff's department accused of rape by the daughters passed polygraph tests. The daughters were unable to give details they might be expected to know of the hundreds of satanic rituals they said they attended. Ofshe, an expert on cults and mind control, retained by the prosecution, concluded that the Satanic cult did not exist and that Ingram, during the interrogations over a period of five months, made false confessions.

In an experiment, he demonstrated the suspect's extreme suggestibility. Ofshe made a false allegation that one of Ingram's sons and one of his daughters had reported that he made them have sex together while he looked on. Ingram said that he could not remember this event. Mimicking Ingram's pastor's requests for information on sexual abuse, Ofshe asked him to "pray on the event" and try to remember it. The next day Ingram reported knowing which son and daughter were involved and said that he had vivid recollections of what had happened. The daughter he had named said that nothing like the invented scene had ever happened.

In May 1989, Paul Ingram pleaded guilty to six counts of rape. Two days later, the prosecutor dropped charges against two friends of Ingram who had been in custody for five months. One man was a retired sex detective in the sheriff's department and the other man was a state patrol car mechanic. Both men incurred expensive legal fees and suffered damage to their reputations.

Lawrence Wright, in his book *Remembering Satan,* describes a witch hunt in Olympia, Washington. He states that Ingram's memories, obtained in questioning by detectives in which psychologists and his fundamentalist pastor participated, became too absurd even for the investigators to believe.

He comments: "At no time did the detectives ever consider the possibility that their source of the memories was the investigation itself— there was no other reality . . . There was another possibility that the detectives did not pursue. From the beginning, both of the Ingram daughters had said that they had sex with their brothers . . . The detectives chose to believe that even if there was sexual acting-out among the siblings, such behavior must have been learned—presumably through abuse by the parents."

Sentencing of Ingram was delayed after Julie received a letter allegedly written by her father. In it he threatened to kill her. Both defense and prosecution handwriting experts agreed that the letter was in Julie's handwriting. In May 1990, Ingram was sentenced to twenty years in prison. An appeal has been rejected by the Washington Supreme Court.

Satanic Group Rapes

A major controversial issue is the incidence of sexual exploitation of children by satanic groups. Some mental health professionals report an astonishing incidence of murder, torture, rape, and other sexual assaults of children by members of satanic groups. The examples they give are almost beyond belief.

Children of members of satanic cults are used as breeders, they are raped, the births are not registered, and the babies are killed in satanic sacrifices. The bodies are not discovered by law enforcement because they are dissolved in acid, cremated, or reburied in a site different from that observed by their mothers.

Many law enforcement officers are skeptical of reports of sexual abuse of children by satanic groups. These officers agree that from time to time a man arrested for rape and murder will say that he was responding to the voice of Satan who ordered him to rape and kill. He is either a paranoid schizophrenic suffering from hallucinations and delusions or an antisocial personality faking schizophrenia in the hope of escaping punishment through a plea of insanity.

REFERENCES

Bane, Vickie.: The darkest secret. *People*, June 10, 1991.

Bell, Stuart.: *When Salem Came To The Boro: The true story of the Cleveland child abuse crisis.* London, Pan, 1988.

Benedek, E. and Shetky, D.: Allegations of sexual abuse in child custody and visitation disputes. In Shetky, D. and Benedek, E.: *Emerging Issues in Child Psychiatry and the Law.* New York, Bruner Mazel, 1985.

Butler-Sloss Lord.: *Report of the Inquiry into Child Abuse in Cleveland 1988.* London, H.M. Stationary Office, 1988.

Carlson, Margaret. Six years of trial by torture. *Time,* January 29, 1990.

Ceci, S.J., and Bruck, Maggie.: Suggestibility of the Child witness: A historical review and synthesis. *Psychol Bull, 113:*403, 1993.

Clare, Anthony.: Need for common sense. *Sunday Times,* (London), July 10, 1988.

Crewdson, John,: *By Silence Betrayed: Sexual Abuse of Children in America.* Boston, Little, Brown and Company, 1988.

Everson, M.B., and Boat, D.W.: False allegations of child sexual abuse by children and adolescents. *J Am Acad Child Adoles Psychiatry, 28:*230, 1989.

Everson, M.D., and Boat, B.W.: Putting the anatomical doll controversy in perspective. *Child Abuse Negl, 18:*113, 1994

Gardner, R.A.: *Sex Abuse Hysteria: Salem witch trials revisited.* New Jersey, Creative Therapeutics, 1991.

Gardner, R.A.: *True and False Accusations of Child Sexual Abuse.* New Jersey, Creative Therapeutics, 1992.

Hechler, David.: *The Battle and the Backlash: The child sexual abuse law.* Lexington, Lexington Books, 1988.

Herman, J.L., and Schatzow, E.: Recovery and verification of memories of childhood sexual trauma. *Psychoanal Psychol, 4:* 1, 1987.

Holmes, D.S.: The evidence for repression, in Singer, J.L. (Ed.): *Repression and Dissociation.* Chicago, University of Chicago Press, 1990.

Jones, D.P.H.: The evidence of a three-year-old child. *Criminal Law Rev.* 677, 1987.

Jones, D.P.H., and Krugman, R.D.: Can a three year old bear witness to her sexual assault and attempted murder? *Child Abuse Negl, 10:*253,1986.

Jones, D.P.H., and McGraw, J.M.: Reliable and fictitious accounts of sexual abuse to children. *J Interpersonal Violence, 2:*27,1987.

Lamb, M. E.: The investigation of child sexual abuse: An interdisciplinary consensus statement. *Child Abuse Negl, 18:*1021,1994.

Loftus, Elizabeth., and Ketcham, Katherine: *The Myth of Repressed Memory.* New York, St. Martin's Press, 1994.

Macdonald, J.M.: *Psychiatry and the Criminal.* 3rd ed. Springfield, Thomas, 1976.

Ofshe, R.J. Inadvertent hypnosis during interrogation: false confessions due to dissociative state; misidentified multiple personality and the Satanic cult hypothesis. *Int J Clin Exp Hypnosis, 3:*125,1992.

Ofshe, Richard, and Watters, Ethan.: *Making Monsters: False Memories, Psychotherapy and Sexual Hysteria.* New York, Charles Scribner's Sons, 1994.

Oulton, Charles.: Cleveland report set to disappoint parents. *Sunday Times,* (London), June 26, 1988.

Pendergrast, Mark.: *Victims of Memory: Incest Accusations and Shattered Lives.* Hinesburg, Upper Access Inc., 1995.

Rabinowitz, Dorothy.: From the mouths of babes to a jail cell. *Harpers Magazine,* May, 1990.

Terr, Lenore.: *Unchained Memories.* New York, Basic Books, 1994.

Thigpen, C.H. and Cleckley, H.M.: On the incidence of multiple personality disorder. *Int J Clin Exp Hypnosis, 32:*63, 1984.
Tylden, Elizabeth.: Child sexual abuse. *Lancet 2;* 1017, 1987.
Wright, Lawrence,: Remembering Satan, *New Yorker,* May 17 and 24, 1993.
Wright, Lawrence.: *Remembering Satan.* New York, Knopf, 1994.

Chapter 7

POLICE RESPONSE TO RAPE

Policemen are soldiers who act alone; soldiers are policemen who act in unison.

Herbert Spencer, *Social Statics*

Controversial issues in the police response to rape that will be reviewed are:

1. Police sensitivity to rape victims.
2. The investigative role of patrol officers.
3. Polygraphing rape victims.
4. Public warnings on serial rapists.
5. Advice on resisting rape.
6. Criminal profiles in the investigation of rape.

There are digressions to review the role of the detective in order to show the complexity of rape investigations and the need to question the victim on many issues that may seem to her irrelevant or oppressive. The disputed usefulness of criminal profiling will be discussed in the next chapter.

The medical examination might not seem to be controversial, but should the emergency room doctor mention the risk of AIDS to a victim who has already suffered so much? There is a brief section on the medical examination to show what a woman faces when she is raped, and a word of caution about some rape crisis therapists.

POLICE SENSITIVITY TO RAPE VICTIMS

Politeness costs nothing, and gains everything.

Lady Mary Montague, *Letters*

Some victims of rape have complained about the insensitive response of patrol officers and detectives. Victims have made similar criticisms of

911 telephone operators, emergency room nurses and doctors, members of the district attorney's office, and newspaper reporters. Some of their complaints have been well-founded, but in recent years training programs in police departments have done much to improve the overall police response to victims of sexual assault.

Police telephone and 911 operators are aware of the need in reports of rape to ask about the victim's medical condition, her location, time of the offense, description of the suspect, his vehicle and direction of travel. The victim is told not to change her clothing, not to shower, and to stay on the telephone until the police arrive.

The immediate concern of officers responding to a report of rape is the well-being of the victim. If she has been seriously injured, a radio call will be made for paramedics to provide emergency first-aid before taking her to a hospital. Even if the patient is seriously injured, an attempt will be made to obtain information that might help identify the suspect and his location. If he is still in the neighborhood, other officers may be able to find him. The immediate welfare of this victim is paramount, but one cannot disregard the welfare of possible future victims.

Fortunately serious injuries are not common (4 percent according to the National Women's Survey), but the victim may well be in great distress. If the patrol officer feels uncomfortable taking the report, the victim will sense this discomfort, which may add to her difficulty in describing the assault. Officers are successful when they adopt a calm, matter-of-fact, frank approach, combined with brief, compassionate expressions of concern at appropriate moments.

It is important to obtain information that may lead to the quick arrest of the suspect. If the victim becomes greatly upset, the officer can shift to a neutral topic and return later to the subject previously under discussion. Answering the victim's questions about the risk of the rapist returning to her home, the need for medical examination, and so on may lead to better rapport. Victims who sense that the officer has their welfare at heart will excuse any shortcomings. If they sense that the officer is indifferent or hostile, they may be resentful and unhelpful.

The Overly Sensitive Police Officer

Police officers faced with a rape victim may not consciously think "What if this happened to my sister, my wife, or my mother?" but their instinctive compassionate response may make it difficult for them to be objective in performing their duties. This may occur even when the victim shows remarkable self composure, but it becomes a much greater problem when the victim is distraught or has been choked, badly beaten, or stabbed.

Homicide and sex crime detectives who become emotionally upset at crime scenes and take their worries home with them at the end of the day are not likely to be effective investigators. A certain emotional detachment is necessary or "burnout" will soon take its toll. A surgeon's clinical judgment may be adversely affected by great distress over patients with advanced cancer, serious burns, or mutilating injuries. Doctors are advised not to treat members of their own family because they may not recognize symptoms or signs they do not want to see.

The patrol officer or detective who is very upset over the suffering of a rape victim may fail to ask important questions and may overlook the significance of something at the crime scene that might lead to the arrest of the offender. If the victim fails to mention that the man ejaculated prematurely, wiped his penis with a tissue which he threw in a waste basket and no inquiry was made by the officer about either the rapist or the victim wiping themselves, the evidence may go out with the trash the next morning, never to be recovered.

The responding officers may overlook warning signs that the victim is not telling the whole truth. Something she said or something at the crime scene that should have alerted the officer goes unnoticed as in the following example.

On a Saturday night, patrol officers were notified by radio of a possible domestic violence and assault that had been reported by a neighbor. At the address they saw a woman on the sidewalk in front of the house yelling for help and crying. She had blood on her face and clothing from head and facial injuries. When a man came out the front door, her crying increased and she began shaking all over. She was taken to a hospital and the man was arrested.

She told the officers that her name was Mary Jones and handed them her driver's license. She met the man for the first time in a bar on Thursday night. After going to his home, she agreed to have sex with him. Later, when she wanted to leave he told her he had a knife and a gun and would kill her if she tried to leave. He tied her hands behind her back with white nylon rope, and held her prisoner for three days. He raped her repeatedly vaginally, orally, and anally. She was blindfolded during the sex with a black bandanna which she said was in the pocket of his suit jacket in his bedroom closet.

On Friday, he injected cocaine into both her arms. When she tried to leave he beat her with his fists. On Saturday, he let her get dressed and after he dozed off she went to the front door and unlocked the dead bolt, but this woke him up and he struck her on the head and face with a hammer. Eventually, about 10 P.M. on Saturday night, she was able to escape from the home.

The suspect, when asked by a detective when he met Mary Jones, replied, "Who is Mary Jones?" On being told that it was the victim, he started laughing and said that her name was not Mary Jones, her name was Betty Wilson and she was wanted on three arrest warrants. He had picked her up on Thursday and they had been partying at his place. On Saturday they went to a laundromat to do his and her laundry, then went to a store before returning to his house. She accused him of looking at another woman when they left the laundromat and this made him very angry. She continued to nag him when they returned to his house and this is when he lost his temper and began beating her.

That night she said "vile things" about his brother and sister and claimed that he owed her $400. She tried to prevent him from sleeping by turning the light on and by opening the window to let the cold air in. He denied hitting her with a hammer, but admitted "beating the shit out of her." He asked her repeatedly to leave and did not hold her captive. He did not sexually assault her and he did not inject her with cocaine. They had shot up cocaine together. She had a house key, that he had given her earlier, on her key ring.

They had known each other for several years and previously had lived together. Two years earlier she had filed a domestic violence charge against him and he claimed that she had lied about him at that time. He was required to attend domestic violence classes and classes on alcoholism.

The detective found that there were three warrants for the victim's arrest, two for drunken driving and one for theft. When shown a police mug shot of herself, she continued to say she was Mary Jones and not Betty Wilson. Yet a driver's license and a social security card in the name of Betty Wilson were in her purse. Two days later, after her release from jail on bond, she appeared at the police building to press charges of rape and assault against her former friend.

She said that she had also been sexually assaulted with objects in her rectum and vagina and that she had bite marks on her crotch and inside her thighs and scratches on her breasts. She was shocked when the female detective asked to see these marks on her. There were no bite marks and no scratch marks. She did have a small bruise above one knee, as well as bruises on her ribs, arms and face. She continued to lie when she appeared in court for a preliminary hearing, telling the district attorney that she had a broken nose and three broken ribs. On inquiry, the hospital reported that there were no broken bones.

In this case, the patrol officers who responded to the crime scene were concerned about her injuries and they did not pick up warning signs that she might not be truthful.

1. The radio call was on domestic violence.
2. The officers did not notice that the picture on the victim's driver's license was not that of the victim, which is not surprising as it was stolen from another woman.
   (a) The victim's face was very different from the face on the license.
   (b) The victim's ears did not stick out at right angles from her head.
   (c) The victim's eyes were brown, the eyes on the driver's license were listed as green.
   (d) The victim's hair was black, the hair on the driver's license was listed as brown.
   (e) The victim looked much older than the woman on the driver's license who was twelve years younger than the victim. Furthermore, the victim looked much older than her actual age.
3. Why would the suspect blindfold the victim when he sexually assaulted her? She had said he spent hours with her at the bar and at his home. He did not blindfold her when she had sex with him with her consent.
4. Why would the suspect, a cocaine user, inject cocaine into another person against her will? That does seem a waste of cocaine.
5. She had needle tracks on her arms from prior use of intravenous drugs. These needle tracks went unnoticed. Chronic drug abusers are not always reliable informants.

THE INVESTIGATIVE ROLE OF PATROL OFFICERS

Patrol officers who interview rape victims should not be restricted to obtaining a brief account of the rape, a description of the suspect, and information that might help locate him. Many police departments restrict questioning by patrol officers and this is the unspoken policy of departments which make no fuss when a patrol officer limits his report to the above issues. This policy is a response to those rape victims who have complained about police officers asking detailed intimate questions. The officer should explain to the victim why it is necessary to go into great detail.

Surely the wish of all rape victims is the rapid arrest and conviction of the rapist. Detectives need the help of patrol officers. An officer should not cut short his questioning either because of official policy or because of his personal discomfort. Every effort should be made to find the suspect without delay.

There are advantages to speaking to a suspect before he has had a chance to dispose of his blood-stained clothing, persuade a friend to provide a false alibi, or move to a distant state. Why discourage keen officers who want to do their duty? Yet one has the impression that some women's groups want to put everything on hold until the victim has been examined in a hospital and interviewed by a victim assistance employee or volunteer. Some rape victim groups even want to postpone the police interviews for several days if that is the wish of the victim.

There are not enough police officers and the sooner a patrol officer or detective is back in service the better. His or her time is ill spent waiting in a hospital corridor or delaying the investigation for several days.

The Police Interview

Initially, the officer asks general questions such as "What happened?" or "What did he do to you?," but eventually he must ask very specific questions because the victim may not volunteer information, for example, on oral sex. Many victims have never heard it called fellatio and may themselves use terms such as head or blow job. Others are offended by such words. Often it is easier for victims to talk about the rape in the first 24 hours after the event. As time passes, they tend to banish all memory of it.

If the victim does not know the identity of the offender, a detailed knowledge of his M.O. (method of operation) may help the detective identify him. Even if the victim knows the man who raped her, knowledge of his M.O. may help solve other rapes that he may have committed. Furthermore at trial the defense attorney will challenge the evidence of an officer who has failed to follow recognized guidelines in questioning the victim. His failure to make appropriate inquiries may result in her assailant escaping conviction and punishment.

Even if the victim had never seen the suspect before, the long amount of time spent with him, which is so different from the experience of most victims of armed robbery, should enable her to notice many small details, even if she was instructed not to look at him. Examples are odors such as gasoline, oil or grease, which might indicate his employment or recent activities.

A vital clue that contributed to the arrest of a serial rapist-killer was a surviving victim's description of a red car with the word "Magnum" on the dash. Only one model Dodge car had that word on the dash. Although she was blindfolded, en route to the release site she peeked out from under the blindfold and saw a Howard Johnson motel.

THE RAPIST'S M.O.

Singularity is almost invariably a clue.

Conan Doyle, *The Adventures of Sherlock Holmes*

Rapists, like burglars, armed robbers and check offenders, seldom commit just one offense. And, like burglars, robbers and check offenders, they tend to keep using the same M.O. There may be changes as the offender gains more experience and learns from his mistakes. Uncommon characteristics are the most important: a bowel motion at the scene or outside the house where the rape occurred, notes left behind, messages on mirrors, theft of unusual items, or an unvarying sequence of events in the sexual assault.

Ronnie Shelton, convicted of twenty-eight rapes and sentenced to over one thousand years, would rape the victim vaginally, then withdraw and ejaculate on the victim's stomach or breasts. He would also frequently masturbate over the victim or between her breasts. He often used the victim's clothing to wipe off ejaculate. Shelton forced many of his victims to have oral sex with him and then insisted they swallow the ejaculate. He would also force them to masturbate him manually. The combination of these acts displayed Shelton's signature . . . Shelton's signature linked him to the twenty-eight sexual assaults. Without the recognition of his calling card with each of these offenses, he may not have been charged and prosecuted to the full extent he deserved (Douglas and Munn).

The Shelton case illustrates the value of questioning rape victims at great length on all the sexual acts even though this may be very stressful for the victim. This questioning may well save many other women from the same fate.

Approach

Hazelwood has described three types of approach: the *con*, the *blitz*, and the *surprise*.

"In the *con* approach, the offender approaches the victim openly with a subterfuge or ploy. Frequently, he will offer some sort of assistance or will request directions. He is initially pleasant, friendly, and may even be charming. His goal is to obtain the victim's confidence until he is in a position to overcome any resistance she might offer. Quite often, for different reasons, he exhibits a sudden change in attitude toward the victim once she is within his control. In some instances, the motivation for the attitudinal change is the necessity to convince the victim he is serious about the rape. Other times, it is merely a reflection of inner hostility toward the female gender. This style of approach suggests an individual who has confidence in his ability to interact with women.

"A person employing the *blitz* approach uses direct and immediate physical assault in subduing his victim. He allows her no opportunity to cope physically or verbally and will frequently gag, blindfold, or bind his victim. His attack may occur frontally or from the rear, and he may use disabling gases or chemicals. The use of such an approach suggests hostility toward women. This attitude may also be reflected in his other relationships with females. The offender's interaction with women in nonrape relationships is likely to be selfish and one-sided, resulting in numerous, relatively short involvements with women.

"In the *surprise* approach, the rapist either waits for the victim in the back seat of a car, steps out from behind a wall or the woods, etc., or he may wait until she is sleeping. Typically this individual uses threats and/or a weapon to subdue her. This style suggests two possibilities: the victim may have been targeted or selected, or the offender does not feel sufficiently confident to approach the victim either physically or through subterfuge tactics."

Statements by the Rapist

Hazelwood has emphasized the need to obtain the actual statements of the rapist. "For example, a rapist who states, 'I'm going to hurt you if you don't do what I say' has, in effect, threatened the victim, whereas the rapist who says 'Do what I say and I won't hurt you' may be reassuring the victim in an attempt to alleviate her fear of physical injury and gain her compliance without force. An offender who states, 'I want to make love to you' has used a passive and affectionate phrase, which is indicative of one who does not want to harm the victim physically. Conversely, a statement, such as 'I'm going to f_____ you,' is much more aggressive verbiage with no affection intended and suggests hostility and anger toward women.

"Compliments directed toward the victim, politeness, expressions of concern, apologies, and discussions of the offender's personal life, whether fact or fiction, indicate low self-esteem on the part of the offender. On the other hand, derogatory, profane, threatening and/or abusive verbiage is suggestive of anger and the use of sex to punish or degrade the victim.

"When analyzing a rape victim's statement, the interviewer is advised to write down an adjective that accurately describes each of the offender's statements, for example, 'You're a beautiful person' (complimentary); 'Shut up, b_____' (hostility); 'Am I hurting you?' (concern). This assists the interviewer in gaining a better insight into the offender's motivation and personality . . .

"By determining what, if anything, the victim was forced to say, the interviewer is made aware of what gratifies the rapist and gains insight into the needs (motivation) of the offender. For example, a rapist who demands such phrases as 'I love you,' 'Make love to me,' or 'You're better than my husband' suggests a need for affection or ego-building. One who demands that the victim plead or forces her to scream suggests a sexual sadist, one who enjoys the total and absolute control and domination involved. If the victim is forced to speak in a self-demeaning or derogatory manner, the offender may be motivated by anger and hostility."

Theft

Hazelwood classifies items taken during a rape into one of three categories: evidentiary, valuables, and personal.

"The rapist who takes evidentiary items—those he has touched or on which he has ejaculated—suggests prior rape experience and/or an arrest history for similar offenses. One who takes items of value may be experiencing financial difficulties, such as unemployment or employment in a job providing little income. The type of missing items may also provide a clue as to the age of the rapist. Younger rapists have been noted to steal items such as stereos, televisions, etc., while older rapists tend to take jewelry or items more easily concealed and transported. Personal items taken sometimes include photographs of the victim, lingerie, driver's license, etc. These types of items have no intrinsic value, but instead serve to remind the offender of the occurrence and the victim."

The patrol officer obtains from the victim a detailed account of the offense, including any acts of resistance and the rapist's response. The detective on his interview makes sure that the above possible acts of the rapist have been covered.

He also will check whether the victim prior to the rape answered any telephone surveys; received obscene, threatening or hang-up telephone calls, notes, or letters; noticed anyone watching or following her; had any repairmen or salespersons in her home; or had any recent disagreements with fellow employees, neighbors or others. Has she previously been a victim of sexual assault?

MEDICAL EXAMINATION OF THE VICTIM

Victims are sometimes kept waiting for hours in the hospital emergency room (ER) and examined without privacy or compassion. They should be given priority over other patients, except those with life-threatening emergencies. They should be in a private room or cubicle. A nurse, social worker, or rape crisis volunteer should be with patient at all times. A willingness to listen to the patient is better than a prescription for a tranquillizer.

The medical examination includes collection of evidence as well as treatment of the victim. The doctor is working for the criminal justice system and should keep a careful record of his examination. In a large city it is better for all victims to be taken to the same hospital where the doctors are familiar with court requirements. This hospital should have sealed Sexual Assault Evidence Kits in the ER. If the taped seal has been broken, this kit should not be used. Even if the victim has washed or douched prior to the medical examination, the evidence should be collected anyway. Evidence includes: blood for blood type and DNA; saliva; hairs in the pubic area; vaginal, rectal, anal, and oral swabs; and all clothing worn by the victim.

Sperm have been found five days after sexual assault in vaginal swabs, two and a half days in rectal swabs, less than two days in anal swabs and six hours in oral swabs, nine hours on lips (Willot and Allard). In some sexual assaults the only laboratory proof will be found in examination of the skin and hair.

In diagnosing and treating sexually transmitted diseases (STD's), most examining physicians prepare cultures to be tested for chlamydia and gonorrhoea at all the sites of assault (oral, anal, and genital), vaginal swabs for trichomoniasis (in female victims), and a blood sample for syphilis. Some ER's automatically dispense prophylactic medication for gonorrhoea and chlamydia because they fear victims may not return to receive the results of testing and follow-up treatment if the cultures are positive for these STD's. Other ER's treat for these STD's only if cultures test positive. For other viral STD's, such as herpes, hepatitis B, and AIDS, there are no preventive treatments (Epstein and Langenbahn).

There is disagreement whether AIDS should be mentioned. The victim has suffered enough already for one day without being confronted with the remote risk of a fatal infection. Furthermore, the test for HIV is for antibodies to the virus and it may be as long as six months before the immune system produces these antibodies. The victim will be advised regarding birth control and will be given, with her informed consent, medication to prevent pregnancy. Many ER's provide a printed handout because victims in this stressful situation do not always remember the advice that they have been given.

Rape crisis counsellors provide emotional guidance and a list of counselling agencies. The volunteer counsellor may herself have been a recent victim of rape. This can be an advantage, but it can also be a disadvantage. The rape counsellor may give her a handout listing all the symptoms of posttraumatic stress disorder. Such a handout may have an adverse effect on suggestible victims.

The Crime Scene

When the rape occurs in the victim's home, the officers will have to search the home. The offender may have left trace evidence or may have stolen items. He may have wiped himself with a tissue and thrown it in a trash can. His sperm is vital evidence. Perhaps he defecated outside the house leaving his *carte de visite odorante.*

THE ROLE OF THE DETECTIVE

It seems . . . to be one of those simple cases which are so extremely difficult.

Conan Doyle, *The Adventures of Sherlock Holmes*

The detective is dealing with the lives of two persons, the suspect and the victim. If the suspect has not been arrested and is not considered likely to flee, he may ask him to come to the police building for an interview. He will not ask the district attorney to file charges until he has carefully reviewed all the evidence. He will talk to both victim and suspect and will review the information provided to him by the patrol officers, and any witnesses. A routine part of any investigation, not just of rape, is to check whether the victim or the suspect has a criminal record.

Even if the victim has lied in her report, she may have been raped. It is not unusual for a victim to be embarrassed over the fact that she accepted a ride from a stranger, so she may say that a car drew up beside her, the driver kidnapped her and raped her. She was raped but not kidnapped.

Systematic application of routine investigative procedures should be combined with an imaginative approach responsive to the special features of the individual case. There is a need for flexibility, a readiness to shift one's focus, to discard a hunch that finds no support or to return to a hunch too quickly discarded. The peril of the preconceived opinion which excludes consideration of alternative explanations is no less dangerous than an unwillingness to speculate until the routine investigation is far advanced.

You will recall the police officer who sought the advice of Sherlock Holmes. The detective drew the officer's attention to the curious incident of the dog in the night. When the officer remonstrated that the dog did nothing in the night, Holmes remarked that this was the curious incident. The failure of the family dog to bark during a nighttime rape led to the arrest of a member of the household, who had disguised his voice and blindfolded the victim.

The combination of sensitivity to discordant circumstances and unrestrained curiosity is perhaps the most important quality of the able detective. Perseverance is essential. An alert mind, retentive memory, and keen powers of observation contribute to his skill. Above all, he must know the minds of men, yet this knowledge surely stems from his lively curiosity and his active search for answers. The investigation of rape is a challenge indeed for the detective who would master the art and science of his profession.

POLYGRAPHING RAPE VICTIMS

Unnatural deeds to breed unnatural problems.

Shakespeare, *Macbeth*

The polygraph machine detects stress by recording changes in the subject's blood pressure, pulse rate, respiration, and galvanic skin response. The lie detector is the polygraph examiner who asks questions and interprets the subject's bodily responses recorded by his machine. Any stress may affect the polygraph recording including factors unrelated to the questioning, for example, the noise of a helicopter flying over the police building. The operator takes many factors into account when interpreting a change in the recording and their possible relationship to the question he is asking.

Critics of polygraph testing point out that it does not always accurately determine deception and truthfulness. Many courts do not permit the results of polygraph to be admitted in evidence. Nevertheless the polygraph has long been used to aid in criminal investigation. Some subjects fearful of taking the test will confess to the polygraph operator before the test has even started.

Most detectives ask relatively few victims of sexual assault to take the test. It is more likely to be used in an acquaintance rape case, when there is no bodily injury, no other physical evidence, no eyewitness, and both victim and witness give apparently truthful accounts of the time spent together. It is her word against his and it is difficult to tell who is telling the truth. Polygraph testing of both the victim and the suspect sometimes provides additional crucial information and one subject may fail the test.

A man beats his wife or girlfriend who then calls 911 and says that she has been beaten. When the police arrive, she adds "Oh, by the way, I was raped." There is something inconsistent about her account. The man tells the police, "Yes, we had an argument, I lost my temper, I hit her, but we had sex voluntarily." In this situation, even though there is bodily injury, a polygraph may show whether the charge should be assault or the much more serious charge of rape. This is not a rare problem.

In any doubtful rape case, if the victim passes the test and the suspect fails, the result may influence the prosecuting attorney to file charges. One suspect when informed that he failed but the victim passed the test, replied, "Hey, it was worth a try, if I beat the polygraph I walk, I had to give it a try." He admitted the sexual assault.

The victim of any crime is offended by a request to take a polygraph exam to test the truthfulness of his or her statements to the police. It is particularly distressing for a rape victim and whenever such a request is made, the investigating detective, not the polygraph operator, should explain the reasons for this request. For example, the suspect has passed a polygraph test or there are puzzling discrepancies in the victim's account of the rape which have not been resolved by discussion with the victim. It is important to describe the test as the victim may have erroneous ideas about a polygraph exam based on watching police investigations on television or movies.

In New York, a task force on sexual assault reported that some law enforcement officials routinely required that a sex assault complainant take a polygraph test before they would start a criminal investigation. Although the practice was not widespread, it was considered sufficiently harmful to warrant legislation prohibiting police from requiring a polygraph test of a victim of a sexual assault crime as a prerequisite to initiating a criminal investigation. California and Oregon also prohibit mandatory polygraph testing of victims of sexual assault.

Michigan has a strict prohibition against even mentioning an optional polygraph test unless the defendant has voluntarily submitted to a test and the test indicates that he may not have committed the crime. In Virginia, the police agency, before asking a victim to take a polygraph test, must tell the victim that the examination is voluntary, the results are not admissible in court, and the victim's decision on whether to take the test will not be the sole condition for initiating or continuing the criminal investigation. This notice must be given in writing.

THE COMPUTER VOICE STRESS ANALYZER (CVSA)

The detective asks the person being tested a series of yes or no questions. The device measures involuntary frequency modulations or micro-tremors in the human voice, that indicate stress. The responses are recorded on a graph. Peaks indicate truth and flat top tracings indicate lies. The interviewer starts with two irrelevant questions, then a key question is followed by an irrelevant question because there may be a delayed stress reaction. For example, "Did you hit her?" is followed by "Is. . . . your birth date?" or "Am I wearing a tie?".

Questions can be asked by telephone, a procedure used by Stasi, the East German spy agency to check on their agents. Taped interviews can also be analyzed. The results are not admissible in court unless the judge, prosecutor, and defense attorney all agree. Unlike the polygraph, the machine is not attached to the subject. The Computer Voice Stress Analyzer is cheaper and easier to use than the polygraph, and training is shorter, one week instead of twelve weeks. The CVSA measures only one bodily response and the polygraph measures three—blood pressure/pulse, respiration, and skin response.

Polygraph operators claim that false results with the CVSA occur more frequently than with the polygraph.

PUBLIC WARNINGS ON SERIAL RAPISTS

When the police become aware that a serial rapist is attacking women in a neighborhood, should they release information on the suspect to the news media? Investigators are sometimes reluctant to do so because they fear that the rapist will just move to another part of town and thereby escape the intensive police patrols established in his hunting ground. Police have an obligation to warn women living in the area, but the information they release should not include material likely to be of evidentiary value.

Thus the news media could be told that a serial rapist, between midnight and 3:00 A.M. is breaking into apartments occupied by women living alone in apartment buildings near the Highline Canal in southeast

Denver between Colorado Boulevard and Bible Park. The public should not be told that he is wearing a brown wind-breaker, black sweat pants, and Nike® tennis shoes. He will get rid of his Nike shoes, which have left a distinctive pattern at some crime scenes and he will wear other clothing. This will lessen his chances of being stopped and questioned if seen by patrol car officers patrolling the area in the neighborhood of the Highline Canal.

ADVICE ON RESISTING RAPE

We give advice, but we cannot give conduct.

La Rochefoucauld, *Maximes*

Many women have escaped rape by: running away; screaming for help; saying they are in their period, are pregnant, or have AIDS; and fighting their assailant. Marchbanks et al., similar to other investigators, found that victim resistance reduced the risk of rape but increased the risk of the victim suffering additional physical injury. Physical resistance or a combination of resistance strategies increased the risk of physical injury. They cited one researcher who reported that women who resisted rape with a gun or knife dramatically decreased the probability of their becoming completed rape victims.

Many police officers are reluctant to tell women what to do if attacked by a sex offender. Women have died resisting rape. They might have died even if they had not resisted, but who is to know? Other women have been seriously injured resisting rape.

An offender raped many women and the only victim to suffer injuries was the one woman who resisted him. She was badly beaten. Her resistance was not in vain, it resulted in his arrest, conviction, and a virtual life sentence. Robert Hazelwood, an FBI Academy behavioral science expert, when asked what advice he would offer to a woman confronted with a rape situation, replied that he could recommend a course of action only if the person asking the question would describe to him: first, the location of the confrontation; second, the personality of the hypothetical victim; and third, the type and motivation of the particular rapist.

Hazelwood and Harpold list various techniques of deterring rapists that have been suggested by others. They acknowledge that these techniques can be highly effective but add that use of the techniques can also have very dangerous consequences. For example, one suggestion is that vomiting, urinating, or defecating will repel the attacker. They mention a twenty-year-old woman who involuntarily defecated and urinated out of fear when pulled from a phone booth. "This so enraged her captors that they began pummelling her and forced her to consume her own waste material. Following this, the four took turns assaulting her sexually. Finally they tied her to the rear bumper of the car and dragged her behind the automobile before releasing her. As a result she suffered numerous fractures and required extensive medical treatment and mental health care."

Another example involved a serial murderer who sexually assaulted and killed seventeen women over a number of years. He did not kill all his rape victims and he told investigators that unless victims met three criteria he would not kill them. "First the victim must have approached him sexually (he frequented areas known for prostitutes). Second, the victim must exhibit some reluctance in performing various sexual acts, and third, the victim must make some attempt to escape. A prostitute victim had met the first two criteria for death, but had made no attempt to escape even though the offender had tried to give her his weapon (unloaded). The victim declined the weapon and stated that she didn't want to shoot anybody, she just wanted to go home" (Hazelwood and Harpold).

RESOLVING CONTROVERSIAL ISSUES

The formation of a Sexual Assault Interagency Council brings together groups concerned over the plight of victims of sexual assault and those who investigate or prosecute sexual offenders. The aim is not to find fault but to find solutions that work to the advantage of both victims and public agencies.

In Denver, the Council includes representatives of RAAP (Rape Assistance and Awareness Program); Colorado Coalition Against Sexual Assault; Ending Violence Effectively; The Gay, Lesbian, Bisexual Community Services; Denver Public Schools; Denver General Hospital; Denver Police Department; Denver Police Victim Assistance Unit; Auraria Campus Police; Colorado Attorney General's Office; Denver District Attorney's Office and their Victim Advocates.

These groups can work together to the advantage of victims. It is a great advantage that members of the group know whom to call in an emergency.

These groups need to publicize the fact that too many rape victims, who willingly accepted a ride from a stranger or went to a stranger's apartment, falsely claim that they were kidnapped. This makes prosecution more difficult and the district attorney may even refuse to file charges. These rapists should not be able to escape punishment.

CRIMINAL INVESTIGATION OF CHILD RAPE

The incest offender is a child molester with a daughter at home.

The controversial issue in criminal investigation of the sexual assault of children is the questioning of children. This issue has been reviewed. In view of the problems involved in children testifying in court, including the stress on them, every effort should be made by the investigating detectives to obtain physical evidence. If the suspect is confronted with convincing physical evidence, he may wish to avoid the unwelcome publicity of a trial on a plea of not guilty. His attorney wants to agree on a plea bargain and the child may never have to testify.

Physical evidence may be in the suspect's home. If the child states where masturbation or intercourse took place, for example, by the child's bed, there should be a search for pubic hairs and semen in all the locations named by the victim. The child may say that the father ejaculated on the cushion at the right end of the couch. Testing may show that semen is on just that cushion.

A warrant for search of the suspect's home should include a search for child pornography such as the magazines *Lolita, Schoolgirls, Boys Will Be Boys, Nudist Angels, Moppets,* and *Nymph Lover;* pictures and videotapes of the suspect engaged in sexual activities with his victims (a videotape may appear to be of some well-known movie, but if it is played for several minutes the movie may suddenly be replaced by scenes of child molesting); and audio tapes.

Includes also computer files, which may list names, addresses, and telephone numbers; correspondence indicating membership in the North

American Man/Boy Love Association (NAMBLA) or other pedophile groups; souvenirs such as articles of clothing; sexual aids such as dildos, vibrators and lubricating jelly; diaries and writings by the suspect on children and sex.

Assigning detectives to watch the suspect for three days may lead to evidence of time spent with many juveniles at roller skating rinks, amusement parks, and arcades. He may have gone skinny-dipping with children in a river. Surveillance photographs will make clear to the court the age range of the children he cultivates. Such evidence weakens the testimony of psychiatrists that he is responding to treatment, that he is no longer sexually attracted to boys, that he is adhering to conditions of parole that he not associate with young children and that he now has a girl friend.

REFERENCES

Douglas, J.E., and Munn, C.N.: Modus operandi and the signature aspects of violent crime. In Douglas, J.E., Burgess, A.W., Burgess, A.G., and Ressler, R.K.: *Crime Classification Manual.* New York, Lexington Books, 1992.

Epstein, Joel, and Langenbahn, Stacia.: *The Criminal Justice and Community Response to Rape.* Washington, National Institute of Justice, 1994.

Hazelwood, R.E.: The behavior-oriented interview of rape victims; the key to profiling, *FBI Law Enforcement Bull.* September, 1983.

Hazelwood, R.R., and Harpold, J.A.: Rape: the danger of providing confrontational advice, *FBI Law Enforcement Bull.*, June 1986.

Marchbanks, P.A., Lui, K.J., and Mercy, J.A.: Risk of injury from resisting rape. *Am J Epidemiol, 132:*540, 1990.

National Women's Survey cited by Epstein and Langenbahn.

Pullitzer, L.B., and Swirsky, Joan: *Crossing the Line.* New York, Berkley Books, 1994.

Willot, G.M., and Allard, J.E.: Spermatazoa—their persistence after sexual intercourse. *Foren Sci Int, 19:*135, 1982.

Chapter 8

CRIMINAL PROFILES IN RAPE INVESTIGATIONS
ARE THEY USEFUL?

JOHN M. MACDONALD AND DAVID L. MICHAUD

Habit rules the unreflecting herd.

Wordsworth, *Ecclesiastical Sonnets*

The word profile refers to a side view of a person's face or a brief description of his appearance, personality, and activities. If you know a man's personality, you can often predict how he will behave under varying circumstances. When a man with a particular type of personality indulges in deviant criminal sexual acts, it is not unreasonable to assume that similar deviant criminal sexual acts may have been committed by someone with a similar personality. Thus sadists commit acts of sadism, and it is likely, but not inevitable, that a sadistic rape murder was committed by a sadist.

We are all creatures of habit. The criminal tends to follow the same routine as he goes about his business. There are changes in his behavior. He learns from experience, but not always. As he gains more confidence he moves from areas he knows well, either from living or working there, to other neighborhoods. A suspect's early rapes tell you where he lived or worked. After a number of rapes he may need more excitement. Rape is becoming commonplace, so his demands and his violence escalate.

His M.O. (method of operation) changes, but not as much as you might expect. A man using a con approach would say to his victims, "I'm looking for my dog. Have you seen a poodle?" Then he started attacking women who were alone in laundromats. Some M.O's stand out. One rapist was attacking his victims in many different areas of town and in neighboring towns. There were two very distinctive features: all his victims were street people, and in every case he gave the victim money before leaving her, presumably to make it look like a whore deal.

153

Diogenes said that habit is second nature. The sex offender's criminal behavior is his trademark, and his trademark should lead him to the penitentiary. That is why it is so important to keep records on sex offenders for many years. I could give many examples of persistence of the same M.O. over ten or twenty years. Here is one example.

A man that I examined after he was arrested for rape in 1974 was sentenced to thirty to forty years in the state penitentiary. In 1993, he was released and in 1994 he was arrested and charged once again with several rapes. After almost twenty years he returned to the same Denver neighborhood. His M.O. had not changed: enters by removing the screen on a window between 1:00 A.M. and 5:00 A.M., wears stocking mask, uses small knife, forces oral and vaginal sex, flees if victim screams or resists, and also leaves if the victim seems too willing to agree to sex.

Basic Criminal Profiling

Whenever a serial rapist begins to make his presence known in a city neighborhood, detectives collect information on him which is reported to the local patrol officers so they can keep an eye out for him. At first this basic criminal profile may be little more than the locations and times of his rapes, a description of his race or ethnic group, age, height, weight, body build, anything distinctive about his speech and appearance, as well as his M.O.

This simple profile may lead to identification of the rapist by patrol officers in the area of his offenses. An officer sees a man fitting the profile walking from an apartment complex at 3:30 A.M. His driver's license shows that he lives several miles away and although he claims to have been visiting a friend in the apartment complex his car is parked several blocks away. Yet there is ample parking space nearby.

It can be difficult to prepare this profile. Victims often vary greatly in their estimates of the offender's height. Some may even disagree on his ethnic group. One wonders if there are two rapists at work in the same area. Yet the overall descriptions of the suspect and his M.O. may suggest that all the victims are referring to the same rapist. There are still problems.

Distinctive features that may be listed include:

- *Locations.* Area of the city, homes, apartment houses, laundromats, streets, parks.
- *Times and Days of the Week.*
- *Suspect.* Ethnic group, height, weight, age, moustache, beard, clothing, ski mask, gloves, body odor, other distinctive features.
- *Victims.* Young, middle-aged, elderly, prostitutes.
- *Approach.* Con, blitz, surprise, request help, offer help, pose as police officer, staged accident.
- *Initial contact site.* Home/apartment, street, parking lot, bus stop, school, park, bar, shopping center.
- *Control.* Weapon, rope, tape, handcuffs.
- *Sadism.* Great cruelty, torture.
- *Burglary.* Method of entry, cut telephone line.
- *Theft.* Items taken.
- *Rape M.O.* Sexual acts, their sequence, words used.

A Criminal Profile

The following criminal profile was based on reports of rapes near the Highline Canal area in Denver.

Suspect Description. White, possibly Hispanic, male, twenties to early thirties, about 5 feet 7 inches, thin build, dark eyes, thick black hair, short hair worn in a helmet style haircut, angular features.

Method of Operation. Enters apartments near the Highline Canal, through sliding glass patio doors or balcony doors, between 12:15 A.M. and 4:00 A.M., armed with a knife. Victims live alone. The dates and locations of the rapes were also provided to the patrol officers, who were determined to catch him.

This very simple profile contributed to his arrest after a 911 report of a prowler outside an apartment house. Several police cars responded and the suspect was seen on a second floor apartment balcony. He dropped to the ground and attempted to run but was tackled and brought down by a patrolwoman. He was charged with six rapes. DNA tests on semen recovered in four of the rapes, matched a DNA test on the suspect. He was a suspect in other rapes in the area, but there was insufficient evidence to file charges.

Although the victims agreed that he had short hair, on his arrest he was found to have long hair which he did up in a bun and concealed under his cap when committing his rapes.

Creative Use of a Criminal Profile

In a quiet, older neighborhood in Denver there were more than twenty rapes by a man wearing a ski mask. Each rape occurred about the same time of night. The man usually entered through a window of a home or apartment of a single woman in her thirties who lived alone. Sufficient glass was removed to permit release of the window catch. The victim would wake up to find him in bed with her. He would cover the victim's face with a pillow, rape her, order her not to call the police for at least two minutes, then leave.

When the victim tried to call for help she could not because the telephone line outside the house had been cut. One woman was raped a second time. There was reason to believe that he had been in the homes of some of his victims prior to the rape. He might go through the woman's underwear and take a few small items. The disappearance would probably go unnoticed or be attributed to the victim putting the item somewhere else. He did not return to some of the houses where he had cut the telephone line and he was always careful to conceal his burglary.

The rapes would stop then start again after an interval that might last months. An alert burglary sergeant noted that there were several criminal mischief reports of cut telephone lines in the rape report neighborhood. He checked these reports and found that they were usually at the homes of single women. A man wearing a ski mask was seen outside one home. The sergeant noticed that one telephone line was cut at an apartment where an attempted rape had occurred one year earlier. He decided to investigate this report himself.

A single woman who lived in the apartment thought the cutting of her telephone line was a prank by some juvenile. The tenant before her had told her about the rape attempt a year previously. When asked who lived in an adjoining apartment, she said a single woman, an airline attendant, who was seldom there. She knew when she was there because she had a red car. The last two nights she had heard someone moving around in the apartment and assumed that it was the woman's boyfriend.

The sergeant decided to check the adjoining apartment and found that the telephone line had been cut. The screen outside the bedroom window had been moved up slightly and when he pulled the screen it came off easily. He checked the window and found a hole that had been made by careful chipping of the glass. This hole was concealed by the lower edge of the screen. It was just big enough to allow the window to be unlocked and the area around the hole had been cleaned of glass fragments.

He was unable to locate the woman who rented the apartment, but the owner let him in to check for a possible burglary. The hole in the window was concealed from view on the inside by a curtain. Any glass that had fallen on the floor during the break-in had been removed.

He found that the renter was skiing at a local ski area so he called all the ski-lodges and left a message at the lodge where she was registered. Late that night she called him and gave permission for detectives to stay in the apartment overnight until the rapist appeared. She thought someone had been watching her and she was afraid to return to her apartment. No one seemed to believe her when she told others about her concern. The next day the sergeant rented a red Subaru car identical to the one owned by the renter.

A woman detective, who resembled the renter, drove to the apartment in the late afternoon. That night she turned off the lights about 10:00 P.M. and lay down under the covers on the bed. Another detective was in the bedroom closet with the door slightly ajar.

At 11:42 P.M. the detectives heard someone at the window. A man in a ski mask quietly slid the window up, bit by bit. Something in one hand looked like a knife. He came through the window, landing almost silently on his hands and feet. He moved very slowly and seemed to be waiting until his eyes became adjusted to the dark. With a hammer in his hand he stood over the detective on the bed. She threw off the covers and the other detective jumped out of the closet. They held the man at gunpoint and seized his hammer and wire cutters. He admitted cutting the telephone line.

READY MADE PROFILES OF RAPISTS

Lecturers from the Behavioral Science Unit of the FBI Academy have described the power-assurance rapist, the power-assertive rapist, the anger-retaliatory rapist, the anger-excitation rapist and the opportunist rapist.

Power-Reassurance Rapist

The power-reassurance rapist is the least violent offender. He seeks to reassure himself of his masculinity and some may be latent homosexuals,

"Only a real man could do this." Usually he is a passive, inadequate person, a loner with few friends and difficulty relating to women. If he dates a girl, she is usually significantly younger than he is. An unmarried man, he resides with his parents or lives alone. A very domineering mother may account for his lack of self-confidence.

He has a menial job that requires little contact with the public, and he sees himself as a loser. He is not athletic and spends his leisure time in pornographic bookstores and movie theaters. There may have been arrests for peeping, obscene telephone calls, or burglary.

Usually he starts out raping women about his own age who live near his home. This is important, because the locations of his first rapes give a good idea of where he lives. He watches and peeps in windows and knows which homes have dogs in their backyard. He picks women who live alone or with small children and breaks into the home between midnight and 5:00 A.M. every seven to twenty days. By wearing a mask or by warning the victim not to look at him, he conceals his face. His weapon is usually a kitchen knife taken inside the victim's home. He warns her not to resist or he will harm her children.

He may also rape in the evening, surprising the woman by jumping from bushes near her home, or he may knock on the door, say he twisted his ankle while jogging, and ask to use the telephone to call his wife. He avoids profanity, asks the victim to remove her own clothing and if resisted, he may leave or negotiate for some other sexual act, such as oral sex. He may threaten her with a knife to get what he wants, but he tends to use the minimum force necessary to maintain control. After several rapes the use of force may increase.

The sexual act usually is brief and he may have quick ejaculation or be unable to obtain an erection. Often he asks for reassurance regarding his sexual performance: "Am I better than your boyfriend? Tell me you like it." After the sex he may spend a lot of time talking to her about her personal life and her day-to-day activities. Before leaving he apologizes for his behavior; later he may telephone her and ask for a date. He will take a souvenir of his visit and he likes to keep records of his conquests.

As he gains confidence, he will move farther from his home in search of victims, and he may rape in the neighborhood where he works. If he owns a car, it will be an older model in need of repair or repainting. He may borrow his mother's car and if he is a delivery man, his rapes could be in widespread locations.

Power-Assertive Rapist

The power-assertive rapist is asserting his manhood and shows a greater level of violence than the power-reassurance rapist. He is an athletically inclined, macho male who drives a flashy car, sports car, or four-wheel-drive pickup and frequents singles bars. He may have been married several times, but his marriages do not last because of his domineering, selfish attitude and his infidelity. He is likely to have a job as a construction worker or truck driver. Despite his dislike of authority, he may seek work as a police officer. Any prior arrests may be for domestic disturbance and for resisting arrest.

He rapes in areas away from his home and work between 7:00 P.M. and 1:00 A.M. every twenty to twenty-five days. The victim may be someone he has not seen before, or perhaps a woman he met in a bar. He may start with a "con" approach, but if necessary, he will resort to physical violence with much profanity and verbal abuse. If he wears a mask or tries to hide his face, he may be living in the area. Usually he rapes when he is out of town and then he makes no effort to conceal his face.

He may rip clothing off, and there may be repeated vaginal sex. Oral sex may follow anal sex. If there is sexual dysfunction, it will be retarded ejaculation. He is impersonal, demanding, threatening, domineering, and degrading. He is interested in himself and not in his victim. Perhaps he has had a bad day at work, he has been drinking, and sees an opportunity to help himself to what he wants. "I was sitting in my car and this bitch walks by." There is no pattern to his rapes.

Anger-Retaliatory Rapist

The anger-retaliatory rapist uses violence far beyond what is necessary to control his victim. His purpose is to punish and degrade women. He is a moody, argumentative man with a violent temper, probably a laborer, construction worker or heavy equipment operator, who may abuse alcohol but is a loner and likes to drink alone. An action-oriented person, he likes contact sports. A high school dropout, he may have been arrested for fighting, drinking, or domestic violence.

The rapes can occur at any time of the day. The offender has been drinking and he has suffered some injustice, real or perceived, at the hands of a woman. He gets even with all women through sexual assault.

He uses a blitz attack, often near his home and perhaps after an argument with his wife or mother. This is important because there may be a domestic violence report. He may have been arrested for domestic violence, speeding, or fighting on the day of the rape. The attack, which may be at any time of the day, occurs on the spur of the moment, and he selects a woman about his own age or older, perhaps someone he knows or just met in a bar.

The attack is violent, and he will use any weapon at hand. He will strike her with his fists or a club, and he may kick her before ripping off her clothing. There is much profanity, and he may continue to beat her during the sexual assault. Anal sex precedes oral sex. If there is sexual dysfunction, it will be retarded ejaculation. Infrequently, death from the victim being slammed against a wall or a car may occur due to a fractured skull or other injury. His aim is to rape, not to kill, but it can happen.

Sadistic (Anger-Excitation) Rapist

The sadistic rapist is the most violent offender and resistance can be fatal. His aim is to satisfy his sadistic impulses. He wants to have total domination and control and he wants to inflict emotional and physical pain. He is probably in his thirties, has a "good marriage," a white collar job, and no arrest record. He is very neat and has a good appearance; his car is clean and well maintained. His IQ is above average and he may have a college education. He likes the outdoors and collects both guns and knives. He also collects detective magazines and bondage equipment.

He may travel a lot and he rapes far from his home and work. He rapes at any hour of the day or night at irregular intervals. His rapes are carefully planned, and he uses a "con" approach. Once the victim is under his control, he blindfolds, gags, and handcuffs her or otherwise places her under his complete control. His weapon is usually a revolver or pistol. He takes the victim to a house or isolated area or rapes her in his van.

He is a sadist and he gets his thrill from her reaction to torture rather than from the torture itself. He rips her clothing, uses degrading language, tortures, and may kill his victim. He may take photographs, tape record, or videotape his crime. There may be much or little sex, but it will probably include anal sex. If he has a sexual dysfunction, it will be retarded ejaculation. The victim may be held prisoner for hours or days. There may be an accomplice that he dominates.

Opportunist Rapist

The burglar who robs a home or convenience store and finds a suitable victim for rape may take advantage of the situation if the victim does not appear likely to resist such an assault. The rape is not planned. He rapes only once and tends to leave evidence at the scene. The offender may be under the influence of alcohol or drugs. He is usually a youthful offender who does not repeat this offense.

READY MADE PROFILES OF CHILD MOLESTERS

Preferential Child Molesters or Pedophiles

These offenders prefer to have sex with children.

Seductive. Usually single, has either not dated or dating has been limited. Lives alone or with his parents. May adopt or try to adopt a child. If married, he has infrequent sex with his wife, for example, once every three months. On those occasions he may ask her to shave her pubic hair, ride a trike and dress like a young child with bobby sox and pigtails. Marriage is often to a woman who already has children. Divorce occurs when all the children are too old for his sexual taste.

He works as a teacher, school bus driver, camp counsellor, photographer, pediatrician, priest, park and recreation director, or similar job. He is a little league coach or does other volunteer work with children.

There are frequent, unexplained moves. He has to leave town suddenly because an angry father has threatened to file charges, notify his employer, or beat him up. His employer, possibly a hospital or church, has told him to leave town after finding out about his activities with children. Premature separation from the military. The reasons may not be clear from reading official records, because there is insufficient evidence to charge him with child molesting.

He has a hobby which brings him in touch with children; for example, he is a clown who performs in hospitals and for social groups or he is a photographer who likes to photograph children at rock concerts and beauty pageants. His home may include toys, games, stereos, and rock posters. Some homes have been described as shrines to children or as miniature amusement parks (Lanning). There are pornographic books, pictures, and videotapes, as well as a videocassette recorder and photographic equipment to record his perverse sexual acts.

He may be a member of NAMBLA, North American Man/Boy Love Association; PIE, Pedophile Information Exchange; PAN, Pedophile Alert Network; Rene Guyon Society or Lewis Carrol Collector's Guild. He may have prior arrests for child molesting, impersonating a police officer, writing bad checks or violating child labor laws (Lanning). He may have been a victim of sexual or physical abuse in childhood.

Sadistic. The sadistic preferential child molester has many of the characterological features of the sadistic rapist who prefers adult victims. Gary Bishop was both a seductive and a sadistic child molester. Some victims he seduced, others he killed.

Situational Child Molesters

The situational child molester does not have a sexual preference for children, but if he is sociopathic he takes whatever is available (your wallet, your car, your wife, or your child). If he is elderly, sick, drunk, physically disabled, mentally disordered, or has an inadequate personality, he may take advantage of vulnerable victims and the vulnerable victim may be a child. Most persons with these handicaps do not molest children. Serial rape murderers who have raped at least one girl under the age of consent include Christopher Wilder and Eddie Kemper who both raped fifteen-year-old girls, and Ted Bundy whose last victim was age twelve. They also killed these girls.

ORGANIZED AND DISORGANIZED SEXUAL MURDERERS

The Behavioral Science Unit of the FBI Academy has described the crime scene and profile characteristics of organized and disorganized murderers. Their findings were based on interviews with thirty-six convicted sexual murderers, including twenty-five serial murderers. Twenty-four were organized murderers and twelve were disorganized murderers. The following description is based in part, not exclusively, on their report (Ressler, R.K. *et al.*).

The Organized Sexual Murderer

He plans his crime carefully and takes steps to avoid detection. Victims, although usually strangers, are carefully selected at a location far from the offender's home or place of employment. Often the victims of serial murderers resemble one another in age, appearance, hairstyle, occupation, or lifestyle. The victims may be hitchhikers, college students, prostitutes, nurses, women frequenting bars, women sitting in cars with male companions possibly in a lovers' lane, women alone in cars, or adolescent youths. The victim is approached in a friendly manner and may be asked for directions or for assistance. There may be an attempt to establish a friendly relationship.

He may claim to be a police officer or other official. Whether dressed in a suit or casual clothing he presents a good appearance and is unlikely to arouse suspicion. Friendly persuasion is replaced by direct orders or the use of force after he persuades the victim to get in his car, or after he gets in the victim's car. The murder takes place at another location.

Victims are often handcuffed or tied with rope. They may also be gagged and blindfolded. Torture precedes rape and murder. He uses his own weapon and is careful not to leave it or other evidence, that might be used to identify him, at the crime scene. The body may be concealed or displayed naked in a posture likely to offend others. Fingers may be amputated to prevent identification of the victim.

Some personal possessions of the victim or a body part such as an ear, finger, or nipple may be taken as a souvenir or as a trophy like the antlers taken home by a hunter. The souvenir later may be sent to the victim's family or given to the police with the explanation that it was found by the side of the road. He keeps a close check on reports of the crime on TV and in the newspapers.

The organized murderer may return to the scene of his crime. If the body has not been discovered, he may move it so that the police will find it. He may volunteer to join a search party for his missing victim and inject himself in the police investigation, perhaps providing misleading information. If the body has been discovered, he may attend the funeral service and later visit the grave. There is no apparent remorse and no change in his everyday behavior.

The organized murderer has an average or higher than average IQ, has graduated from high school, and may have attended college. Although socially adept with a high IQ, his work record may be unsatisfactory because his persistence of effort is not equal to his ambition. Furthermore, he may have been fired from jobs because he does not relate well to people in authority. He may work at jobs below his abilities, for example as a laborer, truck driver, or oil rig worker. Military service may have been in the Marine Corps, Rangers, or Green Berets.

He may have worked as a police officer or deputy sheriff. Failure to obtain employment as a police officer may lead him to become a security guard. He likes to carry weapons, handcuffs, and some type of badge resembling that of a police officer. There may have been arrests for carrying a concealed weapon, assault, assault with a deadly weapon, arson, theft, and impersonation of a police officer. If sentenced to an institution, he is a model prisoner and secures early release because he knows how to manipulate the system to his advantage.

He has a succession of girlfriends because they tire of his selfish, self-centered behavior, but there may be a submissive long-suffering wife who remains loyal to him. His friends may say he is a great guy and fun to be around because of his friendly facade. In sports and other activities he likes to be a star rather than a team player. He drives a car in keeping with his macho image, perhaps a four wheel drive pickup or a late model sports car that is well maintained.

Before the murder there is often stress from problems with money, work, wife, or girlfriend. He may be angry or depressed, but while committing the crime he is, or claims to be, calm and relaxed. Albert DeSalvo, the Boston Strangler, and Ted Bundy are examples of organized rape murderers. At the end of his criminal career Bundy behaved more like a disorganized murderer.

The Disorganized Sexual Murderer

The disorganized murderer is a real loser, a socially and sexually inadequate loner, a high school dropout handicapped by below average intelligence and poor self-esteem. He may have some physical deformity such as a harelip, acne, or a stutter, and he is not involved in any athletic activity. He is a sloppy dresser. His interests are watching TV or reading comic books, and if he has any friends, they probably are younger than he is. He may be described by neighbors as a nice, quiet, shy youth who never bothers anyone. He is a little strange and often is out at night.

Any prior crimes probably are nonviolent, such as window peeping, theft of panties or arson without the use of accelerants. He has a poor work record and often works at menial jobs or as a day laborer. Military service, if any, is likely to be brief. Usually he lives alone or with his parents and has never married. He has no car, may not be able to drive, and is dependent on public transport.

His crime usually is committed at night. The crime scene reflects the personality of the murderer. There is no careful planning, but the crime follows a fantasy that may have been recorded in notes kept in a secret hiding place at home. Perhaps there is a picture from a Playboy magazine with wounds on the body outlined with a colored pencil. There is no thoughtful selection of a victim and no attempt to establish a relationship with the victim.

The first victim is the person who answers the door. It does not matter whether it is a man, woman, or child. That person is cut down, possibly without a word being said. The crime is committed near the offender's home or place of work. Blood is everywhere, the result of a blitz attack with whatever weapon is at hand: a cement block, a knife, but seldom a gun. The victim may be strangled. Blood is smeared on the victim, the walls, and the offender himself. The weapon usually is left at the scene.

There is no torture because the victim is killed immediately, but there is postmortem mutilation of the body, such as removal of the breasts and evisceration. There is no rape, but there is probing of the vagina, insertion of foreign objects, and possibly masturbation over the body. Excessive stabbing or slashing of the body may be accompanied by drinking of blood and eating of flesh.

Bite marks, usually near breasts and genitals, can link the victim to the offender. There is no attempt to move or conceal the body. A souvenir may be taken, such as a ring, earrings, panties, or other article of clothing.

After the crime, the disorganized murderer may become more withdrawn, quit his job, and drink more or use more drugs than previously. Feelings of guilt may provoke return of a souvenir of the crime. He may turn to religion or give himself up to the police. He is less likely to kill again than the organized murderer.

Both organized and disorganized murderers may return to the scene of the crime and visit the grave of the victim. For this reason, surveillance may lead to identification of the murderer. Hidden cameras or voice-activated microphones connected to tape recorders are useful aids. Long after the murder they can be of value. On the anniversary of the killing the offender is likely to return. He may make self-incriminating comments about his rape-homicide and express regret for his crime.

A Puzzling Crime Scene

When the crime scene reveals features of both the organized and the disorganized murderer, for example, a body that has been moved from one location to another, a body that has been raped and subjected to great postmortem mutilation with masturbation into an abdominal wound as well as insertion of a stick in the vagina, it may be that there were two murderers—an organized murderer and a disorganized murderer, each doing his own thing.

INDIVIDUAL CRIMINAL PROFILES BASED ON CRIMINAL INVESTIGATIVE ANALYSIS

FBI special agents on the staff of the Behavioral Science Unit of the FBI Academy at Quantico, Virginia deserve credit for pioneering work on criminal profiling. They use the term criminal investigative analysis because they do more than profiling. In addition to a crime scene assessment and analysis of the crime they provide advice on the criminal investigation, interrogation of suspects, interviewing victims and witnesses, preparation of a search warrant, and the prosecution, including use of expert witnesses.

When requested by a law enforcement agency, the FBI Behavioral Science Unit will prepare a profile in major unsolved cases of selected crimes based on careful study of the crime or series of crimes, including review of crime scene photographs and all available evidence.

These expert criminal profilers cannot give you the name of a serial rapist, serial child molester, or serial sex murderer, but if you give them adequate background information they may be able to give you a profile of the likely offender. The profile may include information on the offender's sex, age, occupation, family background, education, army service, marriage, occupation, vehicle, use of drugs and alcohol, personality, mental state, prior crimes, and choice of weapons.

When there are a number of suspects, information provided by the expert profiler will often single out one suspect. You can now concentrate attention on this person, and question him with great confidence.

Many confessions have been obtained in this manner. Keep an open mind, however, as they may be wrong.

Sex offender criminal profiles or any other criminal profiles should not be mentioned in criminal trials because of the lack of a scientific basis. The presence of many features of a criminal profile in a suspect does not prove any illegal activity.

Critics complain that: (1) The forms that have to be completed on the crime and the victim are too detailed and take too much time to complete. (2) The FBI takes too long to provide the profile and often the case is solved before the profile is completed. (3) The profiles contain too many general statements that would apply to too large a population to be of value. (4) The profiles are sometimes completely wrong, and detectives who place too much confidence in the FBI profiles may stop the investigation of suspects who do not fit the profile.

The FBI does not have sufficient staff to meet all the demands for profiles and priority has to be given to some cases over others. Kidnapping of a child has priority over a homicide that occurred some years earlier. The value of any profile is dependent on the extent and reliability of the information provided to the FBI. For example, the pathologist may wrongly diagnose the cause and time of death. Profilers have to adapt to changes in M.O.'s and crime scenes. For example, more children and adolescents are becoming involved in violent crime. Most detectives appreciate that a profile does not eliminate from suspicion a suspect who does not fit the profile.

REFERENCES

Geberth, V.J.: *Practical Homicide Investigation,* 2nd ed. New York, Elsevier, 1990.

Hazelwood, R.E., The behavior-oriented interview of rape victims: The key to profiling. *FBI Law Enforcement Bull,* September 1983.

Hazelwood, R.E., and Burgess, A.W., Ed.: *Practical Aspects of Rape Investigation.* New York, Elsevier, 1987.

Lanning, K.V.: *Child Molesters: A Behavioral Analysis.* 3rd ed. Arlington, National Center for Missing and Exploited Children, 1992.

Ressler, R.K., Burgess, A.W., Depue, R.L., Douglas, J.E., Hazelwood, R.R., and Lanning, K.V.: Crime scene and profile characteristics of organized and disorganized murderers. *FBI Law Enforcement Bull.* August, 1985.

Chapter 9

DISORDER IN THE COURTS

Any lawyer who says there's no such thing as rape should
be hauled out to a public place by three large perverts and
buggered at high noon, with all his clients watching.

Hunter S. Thompson, *Hell's Angels*

Too many men arrested for rape are not brought to trial. Too many serial rapists are released on probation or receive short prison sentences. Too many rapists who murder are released from prison within a few years and quickly rape and kill again. Legislators have reacted to public indignation by passing new laws, but some of these new laws may lead to a different injustice, the conviction and punishment of the innocent.

In 1993, the Senate Judiciary Committee reported the results of a six-month survey of criminal justice agencies in states that together represent more than 50 percent of the U.S. population. The study showed that in the United States almost half of convicted rapists serve less than a year in prison. Twenty-one percent are placed on probation. Judges and prosecutors often favor sentencing first time offenders, including rapists, to probation on the theory that first time offenders are less dangerous to the community. The report states that a convicted rapist may rape twice, in effect, before he ever sees the inside of a jail cell.

Something is clearly wrong with the criminal justice system. Too many brutal rapists get out too soon. In California in 1978, Lawrence Singleton picked up Mary Vincent while she was hitchhiking. He raped this fifteen-year-old girl and chopped off both her forearms below the elbow with an axe. In 1987, after serving eight years of a fourteen-year sentence, he was released from prison. Eight years for raping a fifteen-year-old girl and amputating both her forearms!

The answer is not long sentences for all youthful and adult males convicted of rape. There are many answers, and one is thorough presentence evaluation of all sex offenders. We need to identify the dangerous rapists early rather than late in their criminal careers. We need to protect women from these recidivists, but we also need to protect men, falsely accused of rape, from arrest and even from conviction.

JUDGES

It may not be the fault of the judge who passed too short or too long a sentence, but it may be. Judges, with or without prior experience in defending, prosecuting, or sentencing rapists do not always appreciate that a dangerous offender may have a good appearance, a steady job, no prior sex offense convictions, a favorable psychiatric report, and testimony from several witnesses, including the minister of his church, on the excellence of his character.

Deceptive Clues to the Offender's Character

Good Appearance. A man's appearance does not tell the whole story; furthermore, appearance at the time of arrest may be very different from that in the courtroom. The defense attorney makes sure that the shoulder length, unkempt hair is cut short. The filthy, torn jeans and T-shirt with an obscene message are replaced by a well pressed, conservative suit and tie.

Steady Job. If a man who reports that he has had three jobs since leaving school is asked to list his first job after leaving school, the name of the company, the date he started work, and the date he left this job and then answer the same questions on his next job you may find that he recalls an incredible number of jobs. A good work record is great but it does not rule out sexual sadism.

No Prior Sex Offense Convictions. He may have been arrested for burglary and rape, but in a plea bargain his attorney's offer of a guilty plea to the burglary charge in return for dropping the rape charge may be accepted by the district attorney. If the suspect fondled a victim he may be charged with assault and there is no mention of sex assault on his record.

A Favorable Psychiatric Report may be from a doctor who is unsophisticated in the diagnosis and treatment of sex offenders. Even if they mention abnormal sexual behavior prior to the offense, they may downplay its significance and if they make a diagnosis of sexual disorder they may claim that psychological treatment is likely to prevent future sex offenses.

Character Witnesses. Many priests are inclined to see the best in people and this can be an asset in their ministry, but may not be in the best interest of potential female rape victims. Family members may have difficulty accepting that their son or brother has the character of Jack the Ripper.

Strange Judicial Decisions

Even experienced judges make strange decisions. In Chattanooga, Tennessee, a man after raping a woman and forcing her daughter to watch, said voices told him to rape. He was found not guilty by reason of insanity and was ordered to undergo out-patient treatment. After he stopped taking medication and attending counselling sessions, his counsellor urged the judge to have him picked up as soon as possible.

The man was arrested but the judge released him three days later with orders for him to attend a hearing the next month. The judge commented, "I think what he needs, he needs a girlfriend because if he doesn't, he's going to have bad dreams again." He told the public defender, "We'll let you arrange a dating service or something." After many persons called his office to complain, the judge changed his mind. He said, "I made an error. I should have taken him into custody and had him examined" (Associated Press 2/19/94).

In Columbus, Ohio, a judge excused the jury and dismissed a twelve-count indictment against a forty-six-year-old man accused of raping an eleven-year-old girl, because a prosecution witness in the case was twenty minutes late arriving in court. By the time another witness arrived in the court, the judge was already explaining to jurors why they were being excused. He said the failure of the witness to appear denied the defendant of his right to a speedy trial (*Law Enforcement News* 10/31/93).

The judge's message seems to be—you can't keep a suspected rapist waiting twenty minutes, or perhaps the message was you can't keep this judge waiting twenty minutes. He claimed that he was not aware that the defendant's previous convictions included prior incidents of child abuse. Even if the defendant had no previous convictions, the judge should not have dismissed the charge of rape regardless of the age of the victim. The judge was suspended for six months without pay, but three months later the suspension was lifted by a state judicial commission.

In Denver, Colorado, a judge dismissed felony charges of attempted first degree sexual assault and second degree burglary against a man who broke into a doctor's home and confronted her while naked. At the preliminary hearing, a detective testified that the defendant admitted that he had a fantasy of having sex with the victim and that he had broken into the victim's house with the intention of having sex with her. However, when he confronted the victim and she became frightened and distraught, he realized that reality did not match his fantasy, and he changed his mind. The victim ran out the front door screaming for help, while the defendant ran out the back door.

The judge found that the evidence failed to show the requisite probable cause that the defendant had intended to sexually assault the victim, rather the court concluded that the defendant had entered the victim's home with the idea of achieving a sexual liaison with her and that such an idea was delusional and "one which a reasonable person would not expect." The judge found probable cause only to the lesser offense of criminal trespass and dismissed the sexual assault and burglary charges. The district attorney appealed this decision. The diagnosis of delusions was made by the judge without benefit of any psychiatric evaluation.

Within a year, before the Colorado Court of Appeals reached a decision on the appeal in 1994, this man was arrested on two charges of breaking into the home of an eighty-four-year-old woman and attempting to rape her. The first time the victim was sound asleep and he landed right on top of her. She fought him and quoted scripture to him. She had a security system installed in her house and her daughter, armed with a baseball bat stayed with her for several nights. The victim was alone when the man used a cinder block to smash a window and break in again. This time he left a few drops of blood and fingerprints which aided in his identification. He was sentenced to thirty years in prison.

Some judges have their own value system on sex offenses against women. In England, a soldier in the Coldstream Guards was given a suspended sentence on appeal after being convicted of rape. His victim had suffered extensive injuries which required hospital treatment. The judge commented, "He allowed his enthusiasm for sex to overcome his normal good behavior . . . and his career would be completely destroyed if this sentence of three years were to stand." Judge John Prosser ordered a fifteen-year-old boy to pay a fifteen-year-old girl he had raped the equivalent of $760 for a good holiday to get over her ordeal. After a public outcry, the Court of Appeal sent him to prison for two years.

A man who pleaded guilty in 1993 to attempted unlawful intercourse was placed on probation for two years. Judge Ian Starforth Hill explained that the man escaped a prison sentence because his eight-year-old victim was not entirely an angel. The child's mother said he effectively blamed her as a slut. The judge did not explain the reason for his comment, but the police said the girl had once been caught with a group of children lifting up their shirts in a garden shed and showing each other their chests. The case was reversed by the Court of Appeal and the man was jailed for four months.

Judge Sir Harold Cassel, before freeing on probation a thirty-year-old man who admitted repeated sexual assaults on his twelve-year-old stepdaughter, told him, "A pregnant wife's lack of sexual appetite leads to considerable problems for healthy young husbands." The judge knew that he would be criticized, but no action was taken against him.

Judge Raymond Dean told a jury in the case of a man charged with raping a woman after a drinking session at his apartment, "When a woman says no, she doesn't always mean it. Men can't turn their emotions on and off like a tap like some women can." When the jury acquitted the man, the judge thanked them and added that he thoroughly agreed with their verdict. The next day after calls for his resignation by women's support groups, Judge Dean said he regretted if his remark had upset anyone (*Sunday Times* 6/13/93).

In Australia, in 1993, a judge in Sydney ruled that a woman who had been raped by strangers had not suffered any substantial psychological effects as she still lived with her boyfriend two years later. He also said that she had partially brought the rape on herself by getting in a car with three men she did not know. Another Australian judge presiding over a rape trial said he had learned from experience that a "no" often meant "yes" (*Law Enforcement News* 5/31/93).

In Italy, in 1994, the Supreme Court overturned the convictions of three men who had been sentenced to over three years in prison for the sexual assault of a girl over the age of fourteen. It was a case of incest that began when the girl was six or seven years of age. Sexual abuse went on for many years and involved several family members and others in a small town of 23,000 people outside of Rome. In ordering a new trial, the Supreme Court said the judges failed to consider the morally twisted climate of the family in determining whether there was any criminal intent. The judges should have considered that the family's environment could be completely different from the rest of Italian society.

The Vatican newspaper called the ruling the result of perverse logic. Tina Bassi, chairwoman of the Chamber of Deputies' equal opportunity committee, described the ruling as shameful. "You can't say no one is responsible just because violence happens in a backward socio-cultural context. That kind of thinking can only legitimize rape" (Press Association 11/6/94).

A CASE STUDY OF
DISREGARD FOR THE VICTIMS' RIGHTS

One Offender—Many Victims

Some judges, in trial hearings, show more concern for the defendant's rights than for the victim's rights. A woman leaving her home one night was attacked from behind as she walked to her car. She struggled and screamed for help. Her assailant, LR, after throwing her to the ground, ran off with her purse. She was afraid to stay in her apartment over the weekend and when she returned she found that the front door had been pried open. Her home had been ransacked and the burglar had taken about fifty dollars, a camera, nightgowns and underwear including panties, bras, and slips. Before leaving, he wrote in lipstick on her bedroom mirror "I'm gonna fuck you in the ass. Be ready—you'll like it."

The burglar, LR, was arrested and charged with this offense. He was also charged with the rape of several women in the Denver metropolitan area. This man would peep into womens' apartments and homes, and break in to steal items, including underclothing. If the woman was home, he would rape her.

A woman who fell asleep while watching television was awakened by this man holding a knife to her throat. He was also armed with a .44 caliber handgun. After tying and blindfolding her, he raped her repeatedly and then made her sit, still bound and blindfolded, on the edge of her bathtub while he showered. During four hours in her apartment he fixed himself a frozen spaghetti dinner and took a nap beside her before leaving her tied spread-eagle on her bed.

Another woman, AB, age thirty-nine, woke up one night to find a man with a scarf around his face on top of her, holding a knife to her throat. He told her to keep quiet, forced a sock in her mouth, turned her on her face, then raped her. Before leaving, he forced her to have both vaginal and anal intercourse as well as oral sex three more times. He was charged with raping her, and at a preliminary hearing, he was released on bond.

Despite the serious rape charges against LR in different jurisdictions, despite a criminal record since the age of fourteen, confinement in a school for boys, an indeterminate sentence to nine and a half years in a state reformatory for burglary at the age of eighteen, and a seven to twelve year sentence to a state penitentiary for burglary and theft at the age of twenty-one, he was released on bond.

While free on bond, LR was arrested for the kidnapping and rape of yet another woman. He also violated this bond by failing to appear in court for trials on charges of rape in two other jurisdictions. It was over a month before he was apprehended in possession of a knife, a .44 caliber revolver, and a list of the names and addresses of persons with the same surname of one of the investigating detectives. Some of the initial names on the list had been crossed off and it appeared that he had been searching for the home address of the detective, with revenge in mind.

It was over two years after the rape of AB that LR was convicted of this offense. Prior to his sentencing, she was asked to complete a victim impact statement. She mentioned her dreaded and deep-seated fear of a return visit by the man who raped her.

She had changed her address, but he had access, through his attorney, to court records showing her new address. She had good reason to fear his return because following his arrest on several charges of rape he was released on bond. He could have attacked her again and he did attack other victims. She described the bond as less than significant.

"In the two years and two months after my assault, I have received sixteen subpoenas from Jefferson County Court alone. These were for preliminary hearings and motions hearings. Many were cancelled at the eleventh hour. Each represents an emotional and psychological jolt to myself and my loved ones. One more delay, after one more, after . . . Physically, emotionally, or psychologically, that's not fair! One must ask where are the victim's rights. I have lost eight months of work and numerous other days for court appearances due to his attorney's legal ploys and stalling tactics.

"For the past twenty-six months he has had every benefit of the judicial and legislative systems, while I, the victim, have had no rights whatsoever, and have really been the prisoner. It was really me on trial, not him. He was entitled to my home address always, and at the time he violated his bond, which made me a prospect to him and a prisoner of my own soul. The fact that my fiance was not permitted in the court during the trial was no more than a ploy to take away some of my emotional and psychological support. He was not a "possible witness" in this case. Where are the victim's rights in this case?"

Sequestration of witnesses, a rule designed to prevent a witness from hearing the testimony of other witnesses before appearing on the witness stand, should be used for this purpose and not as a ploy.

RAPE AND THE CRIMINAL LAW

Laws were made that the stronger might not in all things have his way.

Ovid, *Fasti*

For many years in rape trials, the victim, rather than the alleged rapist, seemed to be the person on trial. The defense attorney questioned the victim at length about her prior sexual experiences and attempted to shift blame from the accused to the victim by attacking her character and by suggesting that she wore revealing clothing, behaved in a seductive manner, or showed poor judgment by hitchhiking or drinking in a tavern. In short, "She asked for it." Using these tactics, attorneys often succeeded in obtaining the acquittal of their clients. Some jurors, especially women, are reluctant to convict when the victim is promiscuous, has illegitimate children, goes out with married men, or has other shortcomings.

Newspaper reports and dramatic accounts of the humiliation of the victim in court discourage women from reporting rapes to the police or from agreeing to testify in court. Many victims, fearful of appearance on the witness stand, are too quick to agree to plea bargains that are to the advantage of the rapist. The plea bargain results in a brief sentence or even probation. Sometimes the accused is even allowed to plead guilty to burglary or some other nonsexual offense so that he has no record of conviction for a sex offense. The next time he is arrested for a sex offense he can claim special consideration by the sentencing judge because "this is his first sex offense."

Reacting to political pressure from feminist groups, attorneys, and other citizens concerned over injustice to rape victims in the criminal courts, legislators in many states replaced laws that allowed evidence of the victim's past sexual conduct to be admitted at trial, that required the victim to physically resist the rapist, and that required corroboration of the victim's testimony. Some legislators also responded to criticisms of common-law definitions of rape that excluded males and spouses as victims and that excluded acts other than sexual intercourse (Spohn and Horney). Some of the new laws, especially rape shield laws, are controversial.

Rape Shield Laws

Rape shield laws are designed to protect women from questioning about their previous sexual history. Under the Illinois rape shield statute, any evidence of the complainant's past sexual behavior is inadmissible, except evidence of previous sexual relations with the defendant. This can lead to injustice. If medical testimony shows hymenal damage; venereal disease; the presence of sperm, blood, or hair in the vagina; or pregnancy following the rape, the defendant's lawyer cannot question the woman about possible sex relations with another man as the source of any of these conditions.

A prostitute claims rape and the defendant tells his attorney that she accused him because he failed to pay her. Yet the defendant's lawyer is not allowed to ask questions designed to show that the encounter was itself an act of prostitution.

Ellis in a review of the Illinois rape shield statute notes that it has significantly curbed the often-brutal treatment complainants received at the hands of zealous defense counsel, but he adds that the statute fails to acknowledge several legitimate purposes for which evidence of past sexual behavior could be used. He recommends an amendment of the statute to permit proof of alternative source of physical condition and proof of motive to fabricate.

In Michigan the defendant may introduce evidence of his own past sexual conduct with the victim *providing* he files a written motion of his intent to do so within ten days after he is charged in court. In a case where the lawyer had failed to file the required notice ten days prior to trial, the jury never learned of the preexisting sexual relationship between the couple. For all the jury knew, the defendant and the complainant were strangers. Technical rules should not be allowed to undercut the search for truth by either the defense attorney or the district attorney.

Nolan Lucas was accused by his girlfriend of grabbing her, holding a knife to her throat, and raping her. He claimed that she accused him of rape only after he told her he wanted to end the relationship. The defense attorney failed to file the required motion in time and the jury never learned of the two-month sexual relationship.

As far as the jury knew, this alleged rape was committed by a stranger. In general, juries more often return a guilty verdict in stranger rapes than in acquaintance rapes. Lucas was found guilty and sentenced to three to fifteen years in prison. The Michigan Court of Appeals reversed the conviction, but the U.S. Supreme Court upheld the Michigan law. Two Supreme Court judges dissented stating that the Six Amendment gives all defendants the right to present all potentially relevant evidence.

Surely in a rape trial the jury should know that the suspect and the victim had a consensual sexual relationship prior to the rape. Justice Sandra Day O'Connor, writing for the majority, said that rape victims deserve heightened protection against surprise. Yet in this case, the victim had admitted the prior relationship in the preliminary hearing. How could she or the prosecutor possibly be surprised by this fact being presented in evidence in the trial?

In 1994, under a bill signed into New York state law, descriptions of clothing worn by rape victims will no longer be allowed at trials. A state senator explained that some people still believe that victims actually provoke the rape by the way they are dressed at the time of the attack.

Many civil libertarians and legal scholars have harshly criticized rape shield laws, especially the more restrictive ones modelled after the Michigan statute, for infringing on the defendant's right to confront witnesses against him and to call witnesses in his own behalf (Spohn and Horney). The Canadian Supreme Court invalidated a rape shield statute similar to the one in Illinois because it violated the defendant's right to a fair trial.

THE CONSENT ISSUE

Faint heart never won fair lady.

Cervantes, *Don Quixote*

In stranger rape, consent is rarely a problem, but when suspect and victim know each other, the issue of consent can be a major problem in court. The defendant admits that he had sex with the victim but claims that it was with her consent. The victim claims the use of force.

Ovid has said that a little force is pleasing to a woman and that she is grateful to the ravisher against whom she struggles. Brantome mentions a lady who confessed that she liked to be "half-forced" by her husband, and he remarks that a woman who is "little difficult and resists" gives more pleasure also to her lover than one who yields at once, just as a hard fought battle is a more notable triumph than an easily won victory.

A certain measure of forcefulness is expected by many women in love-making or courtship. Likewise, the man expects some resistance to his efforts at seduction. It is perhaps not surprising that on occasion misunderstanding results and considerable ill-feeling on the part of the woman may lead to a charge of rape.

Saying "No" and Rape

One might think that saying no continuously means just that. Not so according to a Pennsylvania Supreme Court ruling in 1994. In what was described by the prosecutor as a huge backward step for women's rights, the court decided that unless a woman can prove that she was physically threatened into having sex, she can't prove she was raped. The ruling came on an appeal by a university student who was convicted of rape and indecent assault of a fellow student.

The victim said she went to the man's room looking for a friend. He closed the door and had sex with her. Both agreed that she had continuously said "no," but she did not resist or scream and the male student did not restrain her or verbally threaten her. The ruling found that the male student did not rape her because rape implies force and the woman did not mention in her testimony even the threat of force. The court did reinstate the assault conviction. This seems a strange ruling.

A spokeswoman for the Pennsylvania Coalition Against Rape said the ruling sends a dangerous message to rape victims. "We have been educating people and the police had been educating people not to resist, so you don't face grievous bodily injury."

Saying "No" and Marital Rape

Sex, week in and week out, then suddenly a wife says no, perhaps in the midst of the usual preliminary sexual advances and responses. This occurs not just in marriage but also in prolonged sexual relationships that are neither blessed by the church nor recorded by the civil courts. Suddenly she says no, but the man may be less quick to change gears and go in reverse. Should she press charges? A woman may believe that at any time during sex in a consensual sexual relationship she can suddenly say no and later complain that she has been raped simply because she suddenly changed her mind. Does that make sense?

The Age of Consent

Even if a girl consented to sexual intercourse, the man can be convicted of statutory rape if she was below the legal age of consent. At a time when the age of consent in Tennessee was twenty-one, Ploscowe commented that if Kinsey's research was accurate and if the law could be enforced, this would require the imprisonment of a substantial part of the Tennessee male population.

He cited the case of a man who had sexual intercourse with a girl, not quite sixteen years of age, who was being prostituted by her husband. The defendant was one of several men who had sexual intercourse with her. Neither the girl's marriage, nor the fact that sexual intercourse grew out of a prostitutional situation sufficed to save the defendant from a long prison sentence.

Perkins notes that it shocks the moral sense to see a normal and socially-minded boy convicted of a felony for having been picked up on the street by a common prostitute who merely happened to be under the age mentioned in the statute, particularly if she was actually older than he. Some statutes do not permit imprisonment of men who have had sexual intercourse with the consent of older girls of bad reputation who are below the age of consent.

A review of the age of consent in the United States showed that the range varied from seven to twenty-one years of age until major reforms in the mid nineteen-seventies when the range changed to eleven to eighteen years (Kourany et al.).

Multiple Personality Disorder and Consent

In Oshkosh, Wisconsin, in 1990, a twenty-six-year-old woman with multiple personality disorder said that several of her personalities were raped after she told a thirty-one-year-old man that she had a mental illness. The man claimed that she consented and that he did not know she was mentally ill. It might seem that one of her twenty-one personalities consented. The woman said she had been raped while she was Jennifer, a fun loving, promiscuous, twenty-year-old woman who liked to dance to rock music.

At a preliminary hearing, the judge, apparently believing that only the personality testifying knew what was going on in the courtroom, required the woman to take an oath each time she changed personalities on the witness stand. The lawyers formally introduced themselves to three different personalities. One personality did not know that another personality had been given a glass of water on the witness stand.

When District Attorney Joseph Paulus, seeking a change in her personality, asked her, "Can I have Jennifer, the one who likes to have fun?", she replied, "Of course," closed her eyes and a few seconds later she opened her eyes and said "Hi, Mr. Paulus" in a slightly higher voice. Can you believe this?

Three months later the man was convicted of sexually assaulting this woman. He denied having been warned by others that she had a multiple personality disorder. Doctors testified that she had forty-six personalities. Six of these personalities testified at the trial. A psychiatrist for the defense, who reviewed her psychiatric records, did not believe she suffered from a multiple personality disorder. Later the woman acknowledged having had a sexual relationship with a key witness in the trial, a downstairs neighbor, who testified about her vulnerability.

The district attorney's handling of the case was widely criticized and an advisory opinion by the state attorney general's office recommended that the jury's conviction should be reversed. The judge overturned the conviction, ruling that the defense psychiatrist should have been allowed to examine the woman. There was no retrial because the district attorney told the judge that another trial would endanger the mental condition of the woman. He had consulted three medical experts on multiple personality disorder and they advised against another trial.

Dinwiddie, North, and Yutzy point out that many doubt the validity of the diagnosis of multiple personality disorder and wonder whether it can be distinguished from malingering. They say that it remains to be demonstrated that evaluators can determine whether alter personalities, if they exist, are truly unaware of each other, lack control over other alter's behavior, or are unable to know right from wrong.

Condoms and Consent

A woman in Travis county, Texas reported to police that a stranger walked into her apartment and raped her at knife point. She thought she could avoid the risk of dying from AIDS by pleading with him to use a condom. A grand jury refused to indict Joel Valdez the twenty-seven-year-old suspect. There was a national outcry when a member of the grand jury revealed to a local television station that some jurors believed that the woman's handling Valdez a condom suggested willing participation. A second grand jury indicted Valdez on charges of aggravated sexual assault and burglary.

At his trial in 1993, Valdez testified that he wandered into the woman's unlocked apartment by mistake, became frightened when he heard a noise, and entered the bedroom with a knife he had taken from the kitchen table to defend himself. He claimed that the woman, by supplying him with two condoms, showed that she consented to sex. He testified, "We were making love after that," but he gave conflicting accounts of what happened and admitted that he wasn't invited in and should have gone home. The victim testified that she asked him to please wear a condom because she was afraid of AIDS and didn't want to get pregnant. She said, "I knew there wasn't much that I could do to prevent what was going to happen. I thought maybe I could protect myself from dying from AIDS." Valdez was convicted of raping the woman.

Child Hearsay Exception

The laws of evidence have been changed in some states to protect child victims of sex offenses from the stress of testifying in court. If a child tells someone, a mother, doctor, nurse, or social worker that he has been sexually assaulted, that person may be allowed to testify in court on the information provided by the child. A mother can tell the jury what her daughter told her about a sexual assault by her father, but if father and mother are in the midst of a fierce divorce and custody battle, can one be sure that she is a reliable witness? In Maryland, only a teacher, physician, psychologist, or social worker may testify under the child hearsay exception.

McGough reviewing the special dangers of children's hearsay notes that "Just as there is a danger that the declarant child will lie, forget, or misinterpret what he or she saw, so, too the listener-witness may fail to report accurately what he or she heard. Listeners can suffer from errors of selective hearing just as witnesses are prone to selective observation . . . Distortions of accounts occur predictably at three points: when the real witness relates some of the facts he or she witnessed to the testifying witness; when the testifying witness hears and stores that account in memory; and when the testifying witness summons that secondhand account from memory and repeats it or some version of it in court."

In some states, courts permit the videotaping of an interview with the child. In civil cases, an interview in an office followed by questioning by an opposing attorney is less stressful for the child than questioning in court. The attorneys on either side can make objections which are reviewed later in open court. In criminal cases, questioning, perhaps by a physician, who asks questions suggested by opposing attorneys has been useful in some cases.

Often cases are filed based on information provided by doctors and social workers who have: asked suggestive questions, overlooked inconsistent statements, interpreted recantation of prior accusations of assault as evidence of denial and proof of assault. Yet the defense attorney may be handicapped in his efforts to obtain access to this information before the trial.

Juvenile Sentencing Laws

In some states, juveniles charged as juveniles cannot be held in custody beyond the age of twenty-one. In Warwick, Rhode Island, Rebecca Spencer, age twenty-seven, was stabbed 58 times as she watched TV in her home. Two years later and a few doors away, Joan Heaton and her two young daughters were stabbed to death. Craig Price, the murderer, was only thirteen years old when he killed Rebecca Spencer. At his trial in 1989, he was given the maximum sentence for a juvenile, but by a quirk of the law he went free in 1994 the day after his twenty-first birthday. His juvenile records cannot be released, so if he is stopped by a police officer, a radio check will not reveal that he has killed four persons. He will be legally entitled to buy a gun. Captain Kevin Collins, who investigated the murders, said that Price just loves to kill and there is no doubt that he is going to kill again (Adams).

Before his release, he was convicted of assaulting a guard and sentenced to seven years in prison. Many state laws have been changed to prevent early release of juveniles who have committed murder.

DISTRICT ATTORNEYS

District attorneys exercise much greater power in the administration of justice than is generally recognized. Although the jury decides whether a person is guilty of rape and the judge fixes the sentence, a district attorney decides whether or not the case will ever come before the court and jury. Davis believes that justice is administered more outside the courts than in them and he proposes that the discretionary power of police and prosecutors should be curbed.

"The enormous and much-abused power of prosecutors not to prosecute is almost completely uncontrolled, even though I can find no reason to believe that anyone planned it that way—or that anyone would. Prosecutions are often withheld, sometimes on the basis of political, personal, or other ulterior influence, without guiding rules as to what will or will not be prosecuted, without meaningful standards stemming from either legislative bodies or from prosecutors themselves, through decisions secretly made and free from criticism, without supporting findings of fact, unexplained by reasoned opinions, and free from any requirement that the decisions be related to precedents. Furthermore, decisions of a top prosecutor are usually unsupervised by any other administrative authority, and decisions not to prosecute are customarily immune to judicial review (Davis)."

The decision on whether to prosecute may be made by a young and inexperienced deputy district attorney. Too often a plea bargain offered by the defense attorney is accepted without prior consultation with either the investigating detective or the victim. The detective may have an opinion on the dangerousness of the defendant or may have important information. Too often the district attorney will say that he agreed to the plea bargain to save the victim from the trauma of testifying, even though he did not seek her opinion on this issue. Some states have adopted constitutional amendments requiring consultation with victims.

District attorneys have to be willing to take chances, and not just prosecute those cases that are sure winners.

DEFENSE ATTORNEYS

An advocate must be fearless in carrying out the interest of his client, but I couple that with the qualification and this restriction that the arms which he bears are to be the arms of the warrior and not of the assassin.

Lord Chief Justice Cockburn, 1864

In rape cases there are three defenses: "He didn't do it," "He had sex but she agreed," and "He did it, but he was crazy, out of his mind." Juries have become skeptical of the insanity defense. In some states there is another defense when the victim was under the age of consent. "She agreed and he didn't know that she was only twelve; he thought she was an airline hostess." In rape homicides there is the "rough sex" defense.

"Scorched earth" policy lawyers attack everything, every issue, every witness, including the victim. It matters not to them the harm that is done to those they abuse or the court time they waste, because, if only by chance, the judge may make an error they can appeal or at least one juror may think they have made a point.

There are lawyers who know the best they can do for their client is to accept a plea bargain approved by the district attorney, but they persuade the suspect's elderly parents to mortgage their home so they can fight the case in court, eventually losing the case and ending with a long sentence. They had been offered probation. In order to charge a greater fee, they harassed witnesses at length knowing well that it did not further the case of their client.

RAPE AND THE CIVIL LAW

Involuntary Commitment of Violent Sex Offenders

In some states convicted sex offenders, after serving their prison terms, can be confined indefinitely in a state psychiatric institution if they are considered to be dangerous sex offenders. If the prison staff think a prisoner on his release is likely to rape again, they can request civil commitment of that prisoner.

In Washington, for example, under the Community Protection Act of 1990, prisoners who are determined to be sexually violent predators can be involuntarily committed to a psychiatric hospital after they have served their full prison sentence. A sexually violent predator is defined as someone who has been convicted of or charged with a crime of sexual violence and who suffers from a mental abnormality or personality disorder which makes the person likely to engage in predatory acts of sexual violence. Mental abnormality is defined as a congenital or acquired condition affecting the emotional capacity which predisposes the person to the commission of criminal sexual acts.

This very controversial statute was appealed unsuccessfully to the Washington Supreme Court. The majority ruled that the law is a civil statute and unlike criminal statutes because it was designed to treat rather than punish. Dissenting justices said that "By committing individuals based solely on perceived dangerousness, the statute in effect sets up an Orwellian dangerousness court, a technique of social control fundamentally incompatible with our system of ordered liberty guaranteed by the Constitution."

An American Psychiatric Association Task Force on Sexually Dangerous Offenders has found that such statutes have been troubling for psychiatrists, who have often been left with the responsibility of identifying potential repeat offenders, providing effective treatment, and certifying the safety of their return to society—in the absence of clinical knowledge that would permit those tasks to be performed with any degree of assurance.

REFERENCES

Adams, James. He's killed four, he'll kill again, and he is coming out. *Sunday Times* (London), June 12, 1994.

Brody, A.L. and Green, Richard. Washington State's unscientific approach to the problem of repeat sex offenders. *Bull Am Acad Psychiatry Law 22:*343, 1994.

Davis, K.C.: *Discretionary Justice.* Baton Rouge, Louisiana State University Press, 1969.

Dinwiddie, S.H., North, C.S., and Yutzy, S.H.: Multiple personality disorder: scientific and medicolegal issues. *Bull Am Acad Psychiatry Law 21:*69, 1993.

Ellis, David. Toward a consistent recognition of the forbidden inference; The Illinois rape shield statute. *J Crim Law and Criminology 83:* 395, 1992.

Kourany, R.F.C., Hill, R.Y. and Hollender, M.H.: The age of sexual consent. *Bull Am Acad Psychiatry Law 14:*171, 1986.

McGough, L.C.: *Child Witnesses.* New Haven, Yale University Press, 1994.

Muehlenhard, C.L., and Hollabaugh, L.C.: Do women sometimes say no when they mean yes? The prevalence and correlates of women's token resistance to sex. *J Pers Soc Psychol 54:*872, 1988.

Perkins, R.M. *Criminal Law,* Second edition, New York, Foundation Press, 1969.

Ploscoe, M.: *Sex and the Law.* New York, Prentice Hall, 1951.

Spohn, Cassia and Horney, Julie.: *Rape Law Reform.* New York, Plenum Press, 1992.

Chapter 10

TREATMENT OF SEX OFFENDERS
DOES IT WORK?

He falls low that cannot rise again.

George Meriton, 1683

The rapist seldom confines himself to rape. Sex offenders seldom commit just one type of sex offense. The serial rapist may also expose himself to women on the street. Indeed, as a child he may have started his delinquent sexual career by window peeping and stealing women's underclothing from clothes lines. The father who sexually assaults his daughter may also sexually assault his sons. Treatment of the serial rapist is not just treatment of the impulse to rape; it is treatment of a man with many abnormal sexual impulses.

PSYCHOTHERAPY

The most important difference between a good and an indifferent clinician lies in the amount of attention paid to the story of the patient.

Sir Farquhar Buzzard

Therapists unfamiliar with sex offenders do not always explore the full range of abnormal sexual behavior. "What animals did you have sexual contact with before you left high school?" may be an important question. The therapist needs to ask questions related to possible early sexual, physical and psychological abuse.

Sexual Abuse. What were the sleeping arrangements? Did you sleep in the same room or bed with mother or some other woman? Until what age? Did mother comfort you in her bed when you were upset? Did your mother bathe you? Until what age? Did mother usually leave the bathroom door open and did she ask you to come in the bathroom for whatever reason while she was in the bath? Did mother often inspect your penis? If so why?

What was the attitude toward dressing and undressing in the home? Did you see mother, sisters, or other women in the home in their underclothes or naked? Did you see or overhear sexual intercourse? Did father or mother provide instruction on sex? What did each tell you? Did mother discuss her periods or her husband's sexual performance with you? Was there any pornography in the home? Were your parents members of a nudist organization? As a child were you required to wear dresses and learn embroidery as well as other activities more suited to a girl?

Did you ever live with anyone else while you were growing up? Did anyone else live in the home while you were growing up? (Mother's boyfriend or a relative may have been the abuser and this person may not have been mentioned prior to these questions). Was there any touching, fondling, masturbation, oral or anal sex by someone in the home or vaginal sex with someone? Were you aware of any incest, promiscuity, sexual violence, or sex with animals in the home?

Physical Abuse. Did punishment ever cause bruises, blood loss, black eyes, fractures, or loss of consciousness? Were you ever strapped on the bare bottom? Were you ever struck with a closed fist, choked, burned, or tied up? Were there any threats to harm you, kill you, or cut off your penis? Was a firearm ever pointed at you? If given enemas, frequency? Until what age?

Psychological Abuse. Verbal abuse. Were you ever called a pinhead, shithead, pimp, asshole, queer, faggot, or other abusive term? Was a sister ever called a shit, a fucking slut, bitch, whore, pig, slob, freak, or other abusive term? Were you or a sibling ever told you were not your father's child. Questions to elicit discrimination. Was one child (unlike brothers and sisters) ignored, not given a bike, given cheap presents? Ask questions to elicit parental overcontrol of children. Were there any parental predictions of criminal behavior, sentence to a penitentiary, or even the death penalty?

Sexual Experiences. Subjects for review, in addition to sex relations with animals, include other early sexual experiences, masturbation, homosexual encounters, incestuous impulses and acts, fetishism, indecent exposure, window peeping, theft of women's underclothing, touching or grabbing women's breasts or genitals, the use of a camera, possibly concealed, to photograph women in stores, nude women or women who have been bound with ropes, purchase of pornographic pictures or magazines, threatening or obscene letters or telephone calls to women, fire-setting, cruelty to animals or other behavior which leads to sexual gratification and all manner of homosexual and heterosexual fantasies and acts, including anal intercourse.

Were there any operations on the genitals, such as a late circumcision, an operation for undescended testicles, or a penile implant in adult life. Other topics include parental attitudes on dating, choice of a girlfriend, and marriage. Did the parents attend their son's wedding? What, if any, were their wedding gifts?

Inquiry on these and related subjects should not be limited to one occasion. During treatment the recall of forgotten memories is not always reported to the therapist. Furthermore, as the patient gains confidence in his therapist he may be more willing to reveal facts previously withheld. As he reviews his early childhood, he may select as a scapegoat one parent and make only relatively positive remarks about the other parent. When, as is so often the case in rapists, one parent stands out as having inflicted all manner of psychological trauma on the child, it is easy to overlook the role of the other parent in contributing to the patient's psychopathology.

Clues to significant information not readily available from the patient may be obtained from interviews with other members of the family. It is instructive to interview family members together as well as individually. The most vocal relative may not be the best informant. Frowning, a shift in position or other nonverbal communications of silent members of the family indicate the need for further inquiry, either in the joint interview or in a later private interview.

School, armed forces, and hospital records should be obtained. Police records may reveal information which differs from the patient's account of the rape. A young man charged with forcible rape described at length the compliant behavior of his victim. When confronted by the discrepancies between his version and the victim's, he became very upset and spontaneously revealed for the first time sadistic fantasies of raping and torturing women.

The therapist should not be discouraged by the reluctance of the patient to reveal himself. Slight apparent motivation for treatment and refusal to acknowledge a sexual problem are too often regarded as portents of therapeutic failure rather than as a therapeutic challenge. The patient, whether he seeks help or has it imposed on him by the court, will not find it easy to look at himself and at those childhood experiences which contributed to his abnormal behavior. The recall of forgotten memories may be a painful process, yet the outcome of treatment may depend upon the sacrifices he makes to overcome his impulses to take women by force, rather than by love.

Psychotherapy involves more than emotional support and guidance in a time of crisis. Cure cannot be left to nature and the healing process of time. It is the task of the therapist to make known the unknown, to restore confidence and self-esteem and to aid the patient in his efforts to master his abnormal impulses. The psychotherapist helps the patient to realize that his behavior is influenced not only by conscious reasoning but also by psychological processes within himself beyond his awareness. The patient becomes aware of the never-ending struggle involved in the integration of instinctual drives, the prohibitions of conscience and the conflicting demands of the world around him.

Exploration of the origins of abnormal sexual behavior cannot be accomplished quickly. Nor does intellectual insight necessarily confer control over behavior. The patient needs to gain mastery of his impulses as he copes with day-to-day stresses in his life. He may have to make considerable changes in his manner of relating to others; changes which cannot be made simply by an exercise of willpower. He has to recognize the ways in which he provokes other people to react negatively toward him. His wife may also be in need of psychotherapy, especially when her behavior either provokes her husband's acts of rape or hinders his efforts to reach a more mature level of social adjustment.

Family therapy involving parents and the wife may help resolve long-standing conflicts which continue to handicap the patient. One rapist who had committed many rapes was completely dominated by his mother, who controlled him to an almost unbelievable extent. He was quite unable to relate effectively either to her or to his girlfriends, who differed from his mother in age but not in their attitude toward him. His rapes followed incidents with his mother or a girlfriend which aroused great anger that was not expressed. He would submit to their demands without protest, then drive around in search of a (substitute) victim. In his rapes he controlled his victims as he would have liked to control the women in his life. Although he was of husky build and despite the aid of a gun, he would tie up his victims securely with rope before assaulting them.

Psychotherapists belong to many schools, each with their own theoretical beliefs and techniques. Psychoanalytically-oriented psychotherapy is based on an attempt to seek out childhood origins of sexual psychopathology and to give patients insight into factors which contribute to their abnormal behavior. Critics of such treatment say that the patients continue to rape, but now they know why.

Psychotherapists, regardless of their belief systems, help rapists to look at their disordered behavior, accept responsibility for this behavior, become aware of the suffering of their victims, recognize factors that contribute to their offenses and learn to handle anger, power and control issues more effectively.

Group Psychotherapy

Group psychotherapy has one distinct advantage. New members of the group are confronted directly by other group members whenever they: fail to face up to the fact that they are sex offenders (I didn't rape her, she asked for it . . . she was a prostitute . . . she lied in court . . . I was drunk . . . the jury was biased against me); say one thing in the group and just the opposite in the cell block out side the group meetings; proclaim their undying love for their wives yet treat them badly on their visits to the penitentiary; deny an interest in young girls yet show obvious pleasure in watching young girls on television. Often inmates have damaging information on their cell-mates that is beyond the knowledge of the staff.

PRISON RELEASE PROGRAM

A carefully planned release program is a valuable feature of the cognitive behavioral program described by Marshall and his associates. High-risk offenders are treated in maximum and medium security institutions and are later transferred to minimum security jails where lower-risk offenders are treated. On release to the community, offenders are reassessed and treated while they begin a supervised relapse prevention program.

Any features of the program that might put the offender at risk are identified. "For example, in the case of a child molester, if part of the release program involves living with a family who have children, the treatment group leader may insist on an alternative residence. For a rapist who has characteristically attacked hitchhikers, taking a job that puts him on the road for much of his time would likewise be an unwise feature of a release program. Plans that expose offenders to alcohol abuse, give them excessive idle time, or involve recreational activities that put them at risk, are all challenged and the treatment leader will insist on changes . . .

"They also identify a set of warning signs that might indicate they are slipping back into old ways that put them at increased risk. Some of these signs are observable only to the offender (e.g., fantasizing deviant acts), but most should be observable to others (e.g., heavy drinking, or being unable to account for extensive periods of time away from home)".

HORMONE THERAPY

Depo-Provera® (medroxyprogesterone), a synthetic progesterone, reduces serum testosterone. Clinical effects include reduction of sex drive, sexual fantasies, erections, and ejaculations. Side effects may include weight gain of twenty to thirty pounds, high blood pressure, headaches, leg cramps, fatigue, muscle weakness, depression, and nightmares. An increase in the number of abnormal sperm suggests the need for contraception. The effects on the sex drive are reversible. Stop the drug and the sex drive increases. In long-term animal studies, the drug caused breast cancer in dogs and uterine cancer in monkeys.

Hormone treatment, labelled chemical castration, poses ethical problems. One critic said that it makes a mockery of the whole concept of informed consent when your option is to go to jail or get injected with a carcinogen that can increase the risk of heart attack. Persons not charged with any offense have sought this treatment and convicted sex offenders have requested Depo-Provera treatment as an alternative to a prison sentence.

Roger A. Gauntlett, heir to the Upjohn Pharmaceutical Corporation's fortune (the manufacturer of Depo-Provera), in 1983 pleaded no contest to criminal sexual misconduct for having raped his fourteen-year-old stepdaughter and was sentenced to five years Depo-Provera treatment as a condition of probation. He appealed the sentence arguing that the condition of probation requiring the taking of Depo-Provera is unconstitutional and unlawful, that chemical castration is a form of sterilization which is cruel and unusual punishment.

The Michigan Court of Appeals ruled that the condition of the defendant's probation, that he submit to Depo-Provera treatment, is clearly an unlawful condition of probation because the treatment was still experimental and had not gained acceptance in the medical community as a safe and reliable procedure. The Court was concerned about a number of issues including the effect of treatment on current health, the need for informed consent for experimental treatments, and whether the defendant would be entitled to psychotherapy along with the drug treatment. The full opinion is in *The North Western Reporter* — 352 N.W.2d 310 Mich.App.1984. Gauntlett was sentenced to five to fifteen years in prison.

At present in the United States it would appear that if a defendant agrees to Depo-Provera treatment, a court may order it. If a defendant does not agree to accept the treatment and the court orders it, he would probably succeed in appealing this part of his sentence to an appeals court.

Berlin and Meinecke have described favorable response to Depo-Provera. For example, a sadist who was unable to obtain sexual satisfaction unless he hurt his wife became frightened that he might seriously hurt her or even kill her. He had frequently handcuffed her, shaved her head, stuck pins in her back, and struck her. Since starting treatment there had not been a single recurrence of sexual sadism and conventional sexual activities have become a regular part of the marriage.

CASTRATION

One should not underestimate the importance of the fact that such a compulsory operation is at variance with the prevailing principles of medical treatment. Neither should one make light of the danger of the community losing its soul when it uses such inhuman — or at least according to what is generally termed inhuman — means.

Louis Le Maire

If you cut a man's goolies off he gets quite angry.

Ray Wyre

In 1983, a South Carolina judge gave convicted rapist Roscoe Brown a choice of a thirty-year jail sentence or castration. Brown chose castration, but no surgeon was willing to operate because of a concern over ethics and fear of litigation. In 1992, Steve Butler, a child rapist, asked a Houston judge to let him be castrated rather than sentence him to prison. Once again no doctor was willing to perform this surgery.

Castration is an irreversible operation which is abhorrent to many physicians. The procedure is unlikely to restore the self-respect of the offender; indeed it may lower his self-esteem and indirectly increase any anger he may have toward women.

Although a number of rapists in Europe have volunteered to undergo this operation, they have usually been encouraged to do so by the inducement of a reduction in sentence. Even when there is no promise of a lessening of the sentence, the fact that offenders who undergo the operation obtain earlier release does not pass unnoticed by those who have a prolonged or indeterminate sentence.

Castration does not always abolish the capacity for sexual intercourse. Juvenal long ago reported sexual activity in Roman slaves who had been castrated. Bremer reported persistence of sexual potency from one to sixteen years in thirteen of 157 cases of castration. Sturup, in his review of eighteen rapists castrated in the Herstedvester Institute for Abnormal Criminals in Denmark, reported that two of them were able to have sexual relations three to four times a month following the operation.

One man, several years after his discharge from the Institute, went to a private physician and, by complaining of impotence, obtained testosterone, which reawakened his sexual activity. After being reproached for this, he stopped for a while. Twenty-six years after castration, while on substantial doses of testosterone, he was charged with committing an indecency against a seven-year-old girl.

Six months after castration, a schizophrenic offender attempted to attack a woman visitor to the Institute. Later he hid a knife and then aggressively attacked a young girl who was the dentist's assistant. One man became dangerously aggressive following castration and after eight years was transferred to a mental hospital because of aggressive behavior. It was noted that in one case psychotic episodes were much more severe after the operation.

A survey of 900 men castrated in Denmark between 1929 and 1959 showed that ten, or just over 1 percent, committed sex crimes after the operation. Recidivism rates as high as 7 percent following castration have been reported from Norway and Switzerland.

Heim reported on the sexual behavior of thirty-nine released sex offenders who agreed "voluntarily" to surgical castration while imprisoned in West Germany. In comparison with other studies, it was found that male sexual capacity was not extinguished soon after castration. Eleven of thirty five castrates (31 percent) stated that they were still able to engage in sexual intercourse. The castration effects vary considerably and are not predictable with certainty. The author concluded that the findings do not justify recommending surgical castration as a reliable treatment for incarcerated sex offenders.

In summary, castration for rape is generally regarded as inhumane; it may reduce the sexual drive yet fail to eliminate the offender's impulse to attack women; and it may precipitate or intensify symptoms of neurosis or psychosis. The offender may obtain testosterone to restore his sexual drive.

DOES TREATMENT WORK?

The serial rape offender is like the alcoholic; when he stands before the judge he knows he has a problem and wants help. Patrick McGrath, M.D., former superintendent of the Broadmoor Security Hospital in England, said that the predominant desire of the psychotic and the nonpsychotic sex offender, with very few exceptions, is not to get better but to get out.

In order to get out of the penitentiary or security hospital the sex offender may attend treatment sessions and, after a decent interval, say all the right things. But has he changed? He may be able to beat the plethysmograph test (peter meter) and show no penile response to pornographic pictures. He may take Depo-Provera hormone therapy and attend outpatient therapy sessions but is he still raping or committing other sexual offenses? Do not expect the answer to come from his arrest record. Many rape victims do not report the offense to the police, who have a dismal record of solving those cases that are reported to them.

When reading reports of follow-up studies of treated or untreated sex offenders, one must always keep in mind that freedom from arrest is no proof that the person has not reoffended. I have examined offenders who admitted continuing to rape women even though they were receiving outpatient therapy. Furby, Weinrott, and Bradshaw in 1989 reviewed forty-two studies on sex offender recidivism and concluded that there is as yet no evidence that clinical treatment reduces rates of sex reoffences.

One would not expect a favorable outcome among offenders treated in a maximum security mental hospital. An average 46-month follow-up study of 54 rapists released from a maximum security psychiatric hospital showed that 28 percent were convicted of a sexual offense, 43 percent were convicted of a violent offense and 59 percent were convicted of a subsequent offense of any kind. Sexual recidivism and violent recidivism were well predicted by phallometrically measured sexual interest in nonsexual violence and degree of psychopathy. All sex offenses were counted as violent offenses (Rice et al.).

As many sex offenses do not result in arrest and conviction of the offenders, it is likely that the reoffense rate is higher than the 43 percent reported in this study.

RAPE PREVENTION

A controversial issue is whether women should hitchhike, offer rides to hitchhikers, wear revealing clothing, sunbathe on a front lawn in a bikini. They should be able to do all these things. If they are raped, the fault is that of the rapist not of his victim.

Crime is a fact of life. Both men and women have a responsibility to protect themselves from becoming victims. Police are not on every street corner. Neither men nor women can afford to go around with their minds in neutral. The criminal is likely to attack men or women who seem oblivious to what is going on around them, who walk to their cars from the supermarket without paying attention to the passing parade. Men or women who are alert and ever mindful of danger in this crime-ridden world walk with purpose to their car with the key in hand. They are alert to the presence of strangers, especially those near their car. They turn away and walk back to safety, while keeping an eye on a suspicious person.

Women and men should lock car and home doors. Do not open a door to a stranger. Beware of the man who wants to check the furnace, the telephone, or whatever. Do not leave keys under door mats. Female real estate agents who show vacant homes to male strangers take a risk. Is it worth it? At night draw drapes, curtains and blinds. When with a boyfriend, avoid "lovers' lanes."

If men or women go into high crime neighborhoods to buy crack cocaine, they are involved in the commission of a crime and should be prosecuted for their illegal activities. The thugs who rob or sexually assault them should also be prosecuted. Their victims do not have clean hands.

REFERENCES

Berlin, F.S., and Meinecke, C.F.: Treatment of sex offenders with antiandrogenic medication. *Am J Psychiatry 138:* 601, 1981.

Bremer, Johan.: *Asexualization.* New York, Macmillan, 1959.

Furby, L., Weinrott, M.R., and Blackshaw, Lynn.: Sex offender recidivism: A review. *Psychol Bull, 105:*3, 1989.

Heim, Nikolaus,: Sexual behavior of castrated offenders. *Arch Sex Behav,* 10:11, 1981.

Le Maire, L. *Legal Kastration I Strafferetlig Belysning.* Copenhagen, 1946.

Marshall, W.L., Eccles, A., and Barbaree, H.E. A three tiered approach to the rehabilitation of sex offenders. *Behav Sci and the Law* 11:441, 1993.

Melella, J.T., Travin, S., and Cullen, K.: Legal and ethical issues in the use of antiandrogens in treating sex offenders. *Bull Am Acad Psychiatry Law, 17:*223, 1989.

Rice, M.E., Harris, G.T. and Quinsey, V.L.: A follow-up of rapists assessed in a maximum security psychiatric facility. *J. Interpersonal Violence, 5:*435, 1990.

Sturup, G.K.: Treatment of sexual offenders in Herstedvester, Denmark. *Acta Psychiatr Scand,* Suppl 204, 1968.

AUTHOR INDEX

199

SUBJECT INDEX